W9-BED-092

citygardens

Canadian
Gardening

citygardens

Creative Urban Gardens and Expert Design Ideas

Edited by **LIZ PRIMEAU**   Foreword by **ALDONA SATTERTHWAITE**

McArthur & Company
Toronto

First published in 2004 by
McArthur & Company
322 King St. West, Suite 402
Toronto, Ontario
M4V 1J2
www.mcarthur-co.com

Copyright ©Avid Media Inc. 2004

Editor: Liz Primeau
Design: Carol Moskot Design + Direction
Cover Photo: Donna Griffith

All rights reserved.
No part of this publication may be reproduced, stored in
a retrieval system, or transmitted in any form or by any means,
electronic, mechanical, photocopying, recording or otherwise
without the permission of the copyright holder.

Every attempt has been made to secure permission for
all material used, and if there are errors or omissions,
these are wholly unintentional and the Publisher will be
grateful to learn of them.

National Library of Canada Cataloguing in Publication

City gardens / Liz Primeau, editor.

Includes index.
ISBN 1-55278-407-X

1. Gardening. 2. Gardens--Design. I. Primeau, Liz

SB453.C58 2004   635.9   C2003-907359-9

The publisher would like to acknowledge the financial
support of the Government of Canada through the Book
Publishing Industry Development Program (BPIDP) and the
Canada Council for our publishing activities. The publisher
further wishes to acknowledge the financial support of the
Ontario Arts Council and the Government of Ontario through
the Ontario Media Development Corporation's Ontario Book
Initiative for our publishing program.

Printed in Canada by Transcontinental Printing Inc.

10 9 8 7 6 5 4 3 2 1

This book is dedicated to
all gardeners, but especially
to those who devote
themselves to the honourable
pleasures of creating urban
paradises that rejoice the eye
and refresh the spirit.

[contents

08 FOREWORD by Aldona Satterthwaite   09 INTRODUCTION by Jaqueline Howe

small gardens

12   AN ARTIST'S WALLED
     RETREAT

18   GRAND ILLUSIONS

22   DIARY OF A
     MAKEOVER

30   A GARDEN OFFICE

32   THE ART OF ILLUSION

38   A SHARED GARDEN

40   RECLAIMING THE
     PARKING LOT

44   A DRIVEWAY REBORN

PLANT SOLUTIONS
48   TREES FOR SMALL
     SPACES

PRACTICAL SOLUTIONS
54   SIDEYARD SAAVY

STYLISH SOLUTIONS
58   MINI MIRRORS
60   TAKE COVER
62   UNIQUE UMBRELLA
64   WHEN LESS IS MORE

classic gardens

68 NEW WORLD CLASSIC

74 DIVIDE AND CONQUER

80 BORROWED BEAUTY

88 PEACE IN THE CITY

STYLISH SOLUTIONS
94 GOOD GARDEN BONES
98 CLASSIC REFLECTIONS
100 MIRROR BASICS
102 CONTAINER MAGIC

perennial gardens

108 BREAKING THE RULES

114 THE EDUCATION OF
A GARDENER

120 A FRESH START

PLANT SOLUTIONS
126 PLANTS FOR FOUR
SEASONS
128 THE ROOT OF GOOD
GARDENING
130 YEAR-ROUND GARDEN

family gardens

134 BLURRING THE LINES

140 PARTY GARDEN

146 THINKING BIG

152 COTTAGE IN THE CITY

FAMILY PROJECTS
160 GROWING UP GARDENING

PLANT SOLUTIONS
168 PLANTS FOR PATHWAYS

serenity gardens

174 SERENE AND STYLISH

182 DREAM RETREAT

188 CONTEMPLATING
PARADISE

196 ORIENTAL VARIATIONS

204 URBAN OASIS

GARDEN PROJECT
210 CREATING A POND
216 PLANTS FOR PONDS

218 INDEX
223 CONTRIBUTORS

foreword

I get the pleasure of seeing many wonderful gardens
in my line of work. With few exceptions, though, what I hear most is
"Well, you should have been here three weeks ago when it was really looking at its best," or "Too bad you had to come now—in a couple of weeks
the (insert plant name here) will be in full bloom." Of course, the garden
in question looks like absolute perfection.

I suspect that showing off our gardens is a little like showing off our
children: we want them to be in good looks and on their best behaviour
all the time because we care about them so much. We take the patch
we're given (it usually comes with the house, for better or worse) and
transform it. It's an opportunity to express ourselves, to be close to
nature, to strive for creating the big picture while rejoicing in myriad tiny,
exquisite details. And really, there's little to equal the satisfaction of a
peaceful day spent puttering among the plants in the garden, with the
sun gently warming your back, and the birds and bees companionably
chirping and buzzing all around you (and maybe a cat or dog or two laz-
ing around as well).

This book is an opportunity for you to visit lovely city gardens across
Canada, created under conditions as diverse as our country itself but with
the same passion you bring to your own. Hats off to their owners, who
know that for once their gardens are flawless, thanks to the great photographers and writers who tell their stories in words and pictures, as well as
to Liz Primeau's skilful editing and Carol Moskot's elegant book design.
I hope you'll be inspired.

Aldona Satterthwaite

Aldona Satterthwaite
Editor, *Canadian Gardening*

introduction

One of the benefits of gardening in a city is having the opportunity to share your garden with many more people than just family and friends. It always amazes me how a garden can break down the barriers that exist in a large city.

When I work in my Toronto garden, it provides a wonderful opportunity to chat with my neighbours. We exchange ideas about what worked well this season and share our ongoing dreams about what we want to tackle next in the garden—all part of our great conversations about life.

Amidst the hustle and bustle of city life, we often forget to stop and smell the roses. Gardening, and especially city gardening, is a great reminder to do just that. I was reminded of this recently when I was pruning some bushes in our front garden and a woman who lives in our neighbourhood stopped to chat. I hadn't met her before, but she said she wanted to thank me. I looked at her blankly, trying to recall what I may have done. She could tell I was puzzled and said, "Oh dear, your garden. Every spring your wonderful garden of spring flowers is like a breath of fresh air to this street. It reminds me that there's hope after a long winter and inspires me for the rest of the year. It's just the lift we all need."

We at *Canadian Gardening* want to thank the people who have shared the gardens you see in this book with us. Their creative solutions to Canadian urban gardening are brilliant. Whether your garden is large or small, an area for family get-togethers or a personal oasis, we hope *City Gardens* inspires you. You never know to how many people you're bringing pleasure.

Jacqueline Howe
Publisher, *Canadian Gardening*, President Avid Media Inc.

Great things happen in small spaces designed with wit and attention to detail

small gardens

12 AN ARTIST'S WALLED
RETREAT

18 GRAND ILLUSIONS

22 DIARY OF A
MAKEOVER

30 A GARDEN OFFICE

32 THE ART OF ILLUSION

38 A SHARED GARDEN

40 RECLAIMING THE
PARKING LOT

44 A DRIVEWAY REBORN

PLANT SOLUTIONS
48 TREES FOR SMALL
SPACES

PRACTICAL SOLUTIONS
54 SIDEYARD SAVVY

STYLISH SOLUTIONS
58 MINI MIRRORS
60 TAKE COVER
62 UNIQUE UMBRELLA
64 WHEN LESS IS MORE

an artist's walled retreat

UNDER A CREATIVE HAND, A BILLOWING GARDEN RISES FROM CONCRETE
BY ALDONA SATTERTHWAITE

It's evident in her garden that Erica Shuttleworth likes strong colours and clashing combinations. But separated by the green of foliage, the grey of concrete and stone, and set against the warm brick of her old house, the colours work. Opposite: the side garden, which replaces the driveway
Left: the walled garden, once a garage

When painter/sculptor Erica Shuttleworth returned to Canada after years of living in Florence, Italy, the neighbourhood north of College Street in Toronto's Little Italy felt like just the right place to settle down. In the comfortable enclave of leafy, quiet streets, elegant old houses hunker down companionably with modern condos and well-kept postwar homes. So in 1996 Erica bought her tall, skinny, red-brick Victorian house. The ancient workshop at the rear clinched the deal: it could be con-verted into a spacious studio (she works mainly in encaustic, a messy technique that employs pigment mixed with molten wax).

At that point, thoughts of a garden were the furthest thing from Erica's mind. In any case, the notion was moot, as the property was a concrete wasteland, with the space behind the house and workshop, which could have been garden, completely taken up by a large, 7.5-square-metre garage. "I should have known I'd want a garden, though," she smiles, as her small daughter, Stella, races into the room to show off her bean plants that sprout in pots on the windowsill. "It's osmosis." Erica's mother, Susan, is a talented garden designer, and Erica grew up with a lovely garden and her share of chores to do in it.

So when the bug bit her, she took the roof off the garage to create a walled garden.

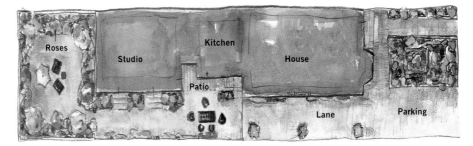

The roof part was easy, but then the real fun began. Erica enlisted the help of strong friends who patiently chipped away at the thick, poured-concrete floor, hauling chunks of it to the dump bit by bit. When enough concrete had been removed to make room for planting beds, 30 centimetres or so of compacted, sour soil was dug out and topped up with rich triple mix. Then Erica installed pea gravel paths with their edges defined by wood. (Some neatly squared-off concrete remains at the centre of the garden; Erica hopes to use it as the base for a seating area and a fountain.)

Next, coping was added to the walls, which were painted lime green. Erica created trellises from the sturdy, square metal mesh used to reinforce concrete—"about $10 for a 4- by 8-foot sheet"—and sprayed them with black, rust-inhibiting paint.

Susan drew up a garden plan and suggested anchors for the garden's four corners—fruit trees (two apples and two pears), yews and Japanese maples, pagoda and yellow twig dogwoods. Yet the garden that evolved is Erica's own.

"Small gardens work best when they have a sense of formal definition," Erica says. She applied some of the principles of painting to her garden, establishing rhythm, colour lines and texture by repeating plants in different areas. Erica likes strong colours and clashing combinations. Her new love is a tiny flowering quince, whose orange-red blooms echo the colour of the stems of a nearby Japanese coral-bark maple (*Acer palmatum* 'Sango Kaku') and provide vivid contrast to the green walls.

The garden is a perfect playground for a small child. "I don't need to childproof my plantings because Stella knows now not to pick the flowers. She loves to help me water the plants and put scraps into the composter."

Erica quickly discovered that her walled garden provides a warm, sheltered microclimate that gives her plants a two-week head start on the nearby gardens of her mother and sister, Laura. She reckons it's Zone 7 at least. "I overwintered a pomegranate outside that's normally considered a Zone 8 plant," Erica says in some amazement. There's a downside to this walled paradise, though. Air circulation is restricted, so plants are prone to mildew and aphids.

"I'm very careful about using chemical controls because of Stella and Flora, our cat," Erica explains. "So now I look for plants that have some degree of disease resistance." Every spring and fall she adds compost to the soil to keep it healthy.

Like most gardeners, Erica's skills have been honed by trial and error. "When I started, all I wanted was some old roses. Then I chose plants by looking in garden centres. I thought variety was the key. But now I'm learning to edit my choices. You can have too much different stuff," she adds ruefully.

This newfound restraint has not made itself felt yet. The garden is crammed with plants—including daphne, Corsican hellebore (*Helleborus argutifolius*), California golden privet (*Ligustrum ovalifolium* 'Aureus'), hardy cranesbill (*Geranium* spp.), delphinium, tickseed (*Coreopsis* spp.), magnolia, 'Pee Gee' hydrangea (*Hydrangea grandiflora* 'Pee

removingconcrete

To remove the old concrete floor, Erica rented a concrete saw, a jackhammer and a dumpster. (You could also enlist the help of strong friends with heavy pickaxes.) Sturdy footwear, work gloves, eye protection and a dust mask are also necessary.

Using the concrete saw, the floor was cut away from the garage wall, leaving a 15-centimetre lip attached. (The steel roof beams left in place help ensure continued stability of the walls; you might want to consult an engineer about your project.) To create the perfectly square concrete pad in the centre of the garden, the space was carefully measured and marked off, then cut out with the concrete saw. The areas of unwanted concrete were smashed up and removed piece by piece. The same method was used to carve out planting beds in the driveway. Check local bylaws before you proceed.

Gee'), lords and ladies (*Arum italicum*), lavender, herbs, clematis and self-seeding sweet pea. Favourite foliage combinations of blue-green, grey-green and chartreuse are found in the hostas, such as 'Halcyon', 'Sum and Substance' and 'Lemon Lime', they are punctuated by the rich crimsons and muted golds of spurge (various cultivars of *Euphorbia*). Erica loves peonies and has about a dozen tree and herbaceous types. Climbing roses soften the walls, among them the rich reds of 'Blaze' and 'Altissimo'. 'Dropmore Scarlet' honeysuckle and purple wisteria twine around the steel beams.

Once the walled garden was established, Erica tackled the space at the south side of the house. She wanted to get rid of the concrete driveway but discovered that it was even thicker than the garage floor, so instead she carved out planting beds, creating a much-used

The front garden is controlled and street-friendly, with a formal stone and slate path, and restrained beds containing a few colourful tiger lilies. Erica is honing her garden style, but her garden is still crammed with plants such as the spiderwort and toad lily, seen left. Far left: wisteria and honeysuckle twine around the entrance to the walled garden.

outdoor living area. The leaky, tin roof over the porch was replaced to provide a sheltered spot, and an awning is planned. "One day, I'd love to enclose this area and have a greenhouse with doors that fold back like a sidewalk café," muses Erica.

Along the side of the house, the no-name roses don't seem to mind being in partial shade. They're joined by others with more distinguished pedigrees, such as 'Pat Austin' and 'Apothecary's Rose', as well as by flowering almond (*Prunus triloba*), a euonymus standard, a lilac transplanted from the garden, burning bush (*Euonymus alata*), viburnum, daylilies, *Pieris japonica*, daphne and clematis. Opposite, the fence is planted up with climbing hydrangea (*Hydrangea anomala petiolaris*), Virginia creeper (*Parthenocissus quinquefolia*) and bitter-sweet (*Celastrus scandens*).

The front garden was the last area to be tackled. As a temporary measure, Erica removed an ugly fence, took up the lumpy grass, added some plants and used old bricks to create a small formal square framed in boxwood. Later, the bricks were removed and the plants set aside. The area was levelled and properly prepared for Erica's first serious garden investment—a Wiarton stone and slate path. That done, the plants were replaced, and augmented with new shrubs, grasses and roses.

Does the garden inspire her art? Erica has always looked to nature for subject matter—fruits, birds and flowers. The canvas she's working on now depicts the skeleton of a small apple tree she lost last year. The painting's translucent layers of wax and pigment palely echo the colour of the garden walls and the shades of the blue-green leaves she loves. ∎

grandillusions

CREATING A BIG, CLASSICAL LOOK IN A SMALL, CONTEMPORARY SPACE
BY PAMELA YOUNG

The pond in the tiny urban oasis runs the length of the back garden and is anchored at the back by a shed that looks more like an elegant guesthouse than a practical place to store garden tools. The niche with a classical urn complements the style of the shed.

In the world of food, fusion is the art of combining traditional ingredients from different cultures to create an original, palate-pleasing dish. In a tiny Toronto garden, landscape designer Ralph Beder has concocted an enticing example of fusion landscaping. A column-flanked classical pavilion is reflected in an asymmetrical, Japanese-style goldfish pool. Vine-covered arbours lend a romantic, old-fashioned air, while ornamental grasses strike a contemporary note. Like a good chef, Ralph paid attention to detail and avoided the extremes of blandness and excessive complexity by blending eclectic elements to create a delightfully pleasing garden.

Ralph says the blend of Eastern and Western influences in this garden reflects the ancestry of his clients. Toronto-born Steve Kemp is of English descent; his wife, Annie, left her native Hong Kong and came to Canada nearly 30 years ago. Before they hired a landscape designer, the Kemps spent considerable time restoring and renovating their cozy 1930s home, adding a sunroom at the back of the house. They didn't have a clear sense of how their garden should look, but they knew they wanted a tranquil retreat. "We told Ralph we'd like to sit in the garden in the evening and forget about everything," Annie says. The designer began to create what he calls "a soft, romantic oasis for two."

The Kemps had erected a lattice-topped wooden fence along the property lines, giving the space a feeling of privacy and enclosure. But they also wanted their 8- by 12-metre backyard to look larger. In response, Ralph set the main part of the garden one step down from the stone patio by the house. "Dividing the space into two areas increases its perceived size," he says. So does axial planning. By inserting a pool down the length of the garden and centring a remarkably elegant shed behind it, Ralph created a visual corridor that draws the eye through the garden toward the focal point that terminates the vista. A view that has a clearly

defined beginning, middle and end creates a stronger sense of progression than a random scattering of elements, says Ralph, and this makes a space look longer than it is. Incidentally, designing sheds that get noticed is one of his favourite strategies. "Everybody needs storage, and an attractive structure becomes a focal point in the garden as opposed to something you try to hide," he says.

The sunroom posed a different design problem. Steve and Annie loved being able to sit inside and look out on their garden year-round. But they didn't like the way the modern, metal-framed addition, with its sloping glass roof, looked beside their traditional house. Ralph agreed that the view of the house from the garden needed work. "The eye travelled right to the top of the sunroom and just kept drifting up," he says. "My intention was to put a cap on the view—to frame it." He achieved this effect by designing a cedar arbour that runs along the top of the sunroom and across the rear of the house, forming a canopy. A thriving silver-lace vine (*Polygonum aubertii*) spills over the arbour and completely obscures the point where the addition joins the house. (The vine is so vigorous that it's cut back frequently to prevent it from overgrowing the sunroom's roof and getting tangled in nearby tree branches.)

Along the south side of the property, a freestanding arbour, also covered with silver-lace vine, shelters one of several seating nooks in the garden. On the fence behind the arbour, Ralph added a lattice backdrop with an urn-framing arch at its centre—a motif as classical as the storage shed's French doors and dentil-ornamented mouldings. To avoid creating a busy effect in a small space, Ralph kept the colour scheme for the garden's built elements simple and subdued. He combined pale yellow and off-white painted surfaces with cedar that was stained dove grey. Light grey Wiarton stone, an Ontario limestone, was used underfoot throughout the garden.

The Kemps' preference for hardy, low-maintenance plants dovetailed nicely with

The garden is a subtle blend of East and West styles in both the structures and plants. The view from the shed, left, shows the arbour across the back of the house, designed to integrate the awkward roofline of the sunroom. Silver-lace also covers an Oriental-style pergola hiding a seating nook at the back of the garden, top right. Beside it, 'Palace Purple' heuchera. Right: Elvis, the family dog, lounges on the back porch.

Ralph's interest in ornamental grasses. "I like grasses—they add an architectural structure for most of the year," he says. "In the fall they turn beautiful colours, and their blooms look interesting when they turn brown." (He suggests that grasses be cut back in spring rather than in fall, to avoid the risk of water seeping into the stems and freezing in early spring, thereby killing the plant.)

To create a tropical feel in the garden, Ralph planted *Miscanthus strictus*—a tall grass with horizontally striped green and yellow blades—close to the back door, where it partially screens the long view. On the south side of the storage shed, he assembled a dramatic grouping of high and low grasses. In back, with vertical green and white stripes, is *Miscanthus* 'Variegatus'. By placing some of it in a planter and more of it at ground level, he achieved greater height range and lushness. Dark red Japanese bloodgrass (*Imperata cylindrica* 'Rubra') in front of the *Miscanthus* creates a striking colour contrast. The bottom step in this staircase of grasses is blue fescue (*Festuca glauca*), which repeats the silver-blue colour of silver firs behind the *Miscanthus*. Between the fescue and the shed, Ralph planted *Heuchera micrantha* var. *diversifolia* 'Palace Purple', a perennial with deep purple-red foliage that complements the colour scheme in the area and provides a contrasting leaf shape.

Elsewhere, two Japanese maples—one of them a cutleaf placed to reflect in the pool—add more rich red tones to the garden. Another beautiful tree is the dogwood *Cornus kousa* 'China Girl', which grows near the house on the north side of the property. Its long-lasting, creamy blooms are followed by exotic berries that resemble tiny, red soccer balls. At the back of the garden on the north side, the white bark of a Himalayan birch (*Betula utilis*) sets off the orange, late-summer blooms of rudbeckia. Placing the dog-

wood and birch on the north side of the garden rather than the south minimizes the shade. This enabled Ralph to plant the grasses and other sun-loving perennials, such as gay-feather (*Liatris spicata*) and thread-leafed tickseed (*Coreopsis verticillata*), that tend to bloom longer and more profusely than many shade-loving perennials.

Annie and Steve had planned to enjoy their garden for many years to come, but a holiday on Nova Scotia's South Shore changed their destiny. They fell in love with the region and concluded they were meant to live there. So they bought an old house in Riverport, renovated it extensively and opened it as a bed and breakfast. Meanwhile, their former home is in good hands. The new owners, Laureen Creighton and Richard Murray, say they were interested in the place as soon as they saw the sunroom and the garden. Moments later, they were standing at the edge of the pool. The goldfish thronged to the surface, expecting to be fed. That's when they turned to each other and said, "We have to have this house." ■

pondtricks

Thick slabs of stone, freshwater clams and queen-size pantyhose helped make the goldfish pool a success. To construct the 90-centimetre-deep pool, concrete walls were poured and a custom-made rubber liner was installed. Landscape designer Ralph Beder specified 6-centimetre-thick limestone coping around the edge of the pool to give it a formal, substantial appearance. But the extra-thick slabs have also proved practical in the raccoon-ridden neighbourhood: they help keep the fish out of reach of the short-armed predator.

Laureen Creighton, who purchased this property when previous owners Annie and Steve Kemp moved to Nova Scotia, says the pool is a thriving little ecosystem. She stocks it with ordinary goldfish, which are hardier than koi and can overwinter in the pond. Water lettuce and North American waterlilies live outdoors year-round with the fish. The more delicate umbrella plant summers at the water's edge, but winters indoors.

Initially, Laureen had difficulty keeping the water clear. Part of the problem was that the pump was at an angle, which meant it was constantly stirring up sediment. Once Laureen insured the pump was upright, the water was much clearer. Meanwhile, she noticed the filter was doing a good job of catching leaves, but it wasn't trapping fish dung and other small matter. After researching pond maintenance at the local library, she added sediment-filtering freshwater clams (and sand for them to burrow in). "The clams seem to have made a difference," she says. But she had even better success with a low-tech innovation of her own. "I pulled a pair of extra-large pantyhose over the filter and tied a knot at the top," she says, laughing. "It works great."

diaryof
amakeover

FROM UNDERUSED SIDEYARD TO WELCOMING SITTING AREA BY BECKIE FOX

The fenced-in sideyard, seen at left before the redesign, was a utilitarian spot that housed a rain barrel and two compost bins, as well as offering the family dog, Holly, a place to glimpse passersby. A year later, the same area is a private garden surrounded by cool greenery.

After gardening on the same suburban corner in Unionville, Ontario, for more than a dozen years, I thought I'd run out of space—until I took another look at our unused sideyard. The small, rectangular area on the east side of the house contained mainly thin grass—made thinner by our dog, Holly, as she dashed along the fence trying to catch a glimpse of passersby— plus the greedy roots of a Norway maple. Two compost bins next to the house were

the most compelling reasons to visit the area. The space was smallish and secluded. It was bounded by the house on one side and a 180-centimetre fence with a gate on two others, which enclosed it from the street and the front yard, and it was open to the back garden. Because the spot faced due east, it sat in cool shade in the afternoon when the back garden, where we had built a large patio several years ago, baked in the sun.

Realizing the 5-metre by 6-metre area had potential didn't help me tap into it, even though I'm a long-time gardener. I knew I wanted a sitting area in verdant tones to reinforce the cool shade, an ideal spot for one or two people with wine to drink and books to read. Grass wasn't imperative, but an aesthetic way to keep Holly from romping through the plants definitely was. So I consulted a landscape architect.

His plan involved a large water feature, a big patio and a bench facing the house. A tall screen at the open end, running from the fence to the house, would keep the dog out. His ideas were exciting, but too grand for our informal garden. I couldn't justify a pond in a part of the garden visible only from the dining room, and we already had a large patio. A bench facing the brick wall of the house didn't seem logical. I realized that with a budget of about $3,000 I couldn't expect a mini Versailles, or a plan and a project manager. But advice on plants, scale, building materials (if applicable) and positioning would be useful.

I asked Toronto horticulturist and landscape designer Judith Adam to come for a look-see early the following spring. Judith works on large- and small-scale projects, with large- and small-scale budgets, and she acts as a consultant for people who merely want advice and ideas. Her consulting fee is based on a one-time visit; if she's hired as a project manager for a garden installation, she charges a percentage of the project's cost.

"Loads of space," she said optimistically as she looked over the area, tsk-tsking the proximity of the Norway maple all the while. But despite the maple she saw potential. Her first suggestion was to plant three tall ornamental pears just inside the fence on the street side, visible from the bay window of the dining room, to add privacy, extend the eye upward and provide pretty white blooms in spring. Ornamental pears have multiple-season interest—an important considera- tion when choosing plants for a small space. As well as flowers in spring, the trees bear glossy green leaves that turn a rich, bronzy purple in fall. She recom- mended the cultivar 'Chanticleer', which has a columnar form, because the trees can be planted closer together than orna-

mental pears such as 'Bradford'. "Try to find specimens that haven't been pruned high," she advised. "They'll have more of a screening effect."

The prime spot for the private seating area I envisioned? A small patio close to the centre of the rectangular space, with a bench looking out toward the main planting area near the fence. Because the patio in the back garden is made of concrete-brick pavers, Judith thought another brick patio would be too much, especially with a huge wall of house brick looming over it. Stepping-stone paths of flagstone lead away from the backyard patio, so she suggested a closely laid flagstone patio in the side garden to blend in with existing materials. Flagstone is more expensive than pavers, but the patio would be only 2.4 metres by 2.4 metres, and because it's a main architectural feature the extra expense would be worth it. (I wonder how often the phrase "it's worth it" is used in renovation discussions.) Two stepping-stone paths would also be needed: one leads to the existing gate to the front yard, the other to the rear garden. Judith suggested another small tree—an upright, lime green cutleaf Japanese maple—next to the house. Its lacy form would contrast with the Boston ivy on the wall behind it.

And we couldn't forget one of the reasons for the side garden's makeover: our rambunctious dog. Judith thought a waist-high, open trellis fence with an arch over the gate would be both attractive and practical. Trellis with openings of at least

15 centimetres wouldn't block the view, but it would keep Holly from trampling the new beds of perennials I coveted.

In May 1998, the crew from a landscaping company removed the thin grass and some overgrown Japanese kerria and burning bushes, and spread several inches of triple mix (topsoil, peat moss and composted manure) over the planting areas. Because the soil is heavy clay and it hadn't been improved over the years, we added extra manure and bone meal to the mix. At the same time, the three pear trees and the Japanese maple were planted and the compost bins were moved to another part of the property.

In mid-June, the patio and two paths were laid. Watching a skilled stonemason in action for a day makes you realize that some jobs are best left to professionals. Admittedly, it's a small patio, but the precision with which it was laid makes its impact that much greater.

Now I could begin planting the shrubs, perennials, vines and groundcovers I'd been accumulating while waiting for the patio to be installed. Most of the garden, which is in Zone 5, receives sun until about 1 p.m., but some beds get only three or four hours. Very little light makes its way to the ground under the

For good drainage and some flexibility, the patio flagstones were installed on an underlayer of gravel topped with stone screenings and then fine sand. Stones were tightly spaced, which meant chiselling to get the right fit and a random pattern. A rubber mallet was used to thump the stones into place, and frequent readings with a level verified that the pathway stayed smooth and sloped gently away from the house. The pathway stones were placed to fit the stride of an average adult, and one was set beside the rain barrel to hold a watering can. Opposite, looking through the arched back gate toward the front entrance

Pagoda dogwood

Auricula primroses

Joe-Pye weed

Mock orange

White bleeding heart over-planted with cleome

Boston Ivy

Cutleaf Japanese maple

White browallia

Scotch moss

Creeping thyme

'Green Velvet' boxwood

Columbine

Dwarf goatsbeard

'Krossa Regal' hosta

'Chocolate Ruffles' coralbells

'Fairy's Joke' hair grass

pagoda dogwood, which is where many of the true shade lovers—wild ginger, ferns, hostas—reside.

Other than the four new trees, plus the existing pagoda dogwood, a large blue hosta and a mock orange shrub, I had a clean slate. Naturally, I had to consider my garden's conditions: it's in Zone 5 and most of it receives morning sun only. Otherwise, it was a chance to follow a cohesive design, and I resolved not to plant just one or two of this or that variety.

In the end, limiting my plant palette proved unpalatable, and discipline flew out the door. I did set a few parameters—to stick with varieties I'd never grown before, but no variegated foliage because the rest of the garden is replete with it. Eventually, I based my choices on leaf colour and shape, and a colour scheme of white, pink and dark burgundy/purple. I favoured foliage that was lime green (Scotch moss, 'Sum and Substance' hosta), deep purple ('Chocolate Ruffles' coralbells and bugleweed) and blue-green (*Rosa glauca*, Arctic willow). Plants with unusual or dramatic leaf shapes, such as rodgersia and Solomon's–seal, also found a spot. Two ornamental grasses add a wispy texture and rustle in the slightest breeze.

I did most of the planting in one day (the beds had already been dug and levelled by the landscaping crew)—on June 21, the longest day of the year, thank goodness. My notes say: "Started planting at 8:30 a.m.; stopped when it got dark.

plantlist

TREES AND SHRUBS
- Cutleaf Japanese maple (*Acer dissectum palmatum* 'Seiryu')
- Saskatoon berry (*Amelanchier alnifolia* 'Smokey')
- *Buxus* 'Green Velvet', a hardy, fast-growing boxwood
- Pagoda dogwood (*Cornus alternifolia*)
- *Daphne mezereum alba*
- Hydrangea (*H. paniculata* 'Unique')
- Mock orange (*Philadelphus* spp.)
- *Pieris japonica*
- Ornamental pear (*Pyrus calleryana* 'Chanticleer')
- *Rosa glauca*, *R. rugosa* 'Henry Hudson' and a hybrid perpetual, 'Mrs. John Laing'
- Arctic willow (*Salix purpurea* 'Gracilis')
- *Sophora japonica* 'Pendula'
- Spirea (*Spiraea japonica* 'Shirobana')
- Yew (*Taxus media* 'Densiformis' and 'Hicksii')

VINES
- *Akebia quinata*
- *Clematis viticella* 'Madame Julia Correvon'
- Climbing hydrangea (*H. petiolaris*)

PERENNIALS
- Columbine (*Aquilegia vulgaris*)
- Bearberry (*Arctostaphylos uva-ursi* 'Vancouver Jade')
- Dwarf goatsbeard (*Aruncus aethusifolius*)
- Wild ginger (*Asarum canadense*)
- White false indigo (*Baptisia lactea*)
- Northern sea oats (*Chasmanthium latifolium*)
- Snakeroot (*Cimicifuga racemosa*, *C. simplex* and *C. simplex* 'Brunette')
- Hair grass (*Deschampsia vivipara* 'Fairy's Joke')
- Ferns, including autumn fern (*Dryopteris erythrosora*),
- Japanese beech fern (*Thelypteris decur-sive-pinnata*), berry bladder fern (*Cystopteris bulbifera*)
- Bleeding heart (*Dicentra spectabilis alba*)
- Joe-Pye weed (*Eupatorium fistulosum* 'Gateway')
- *Helleborus atrorubens* and *H. niger*
- Coralbells (*Heuchera* 'Strawberry Swirl' and 'Chocolate Ruffles')
- Hostas, including 'Halcyon', 'Sum and Substance', 'Krossa Regal', 'Oriana' and 'Janet'
- Jacob's ladder (*Polemonium caeruleum* 'Album')
- Solomon's seal (*Polygonatum multiflorum*)
- Primulas (*P. denticulata*, *P. auricula*, *P. bullesiana*)
- Fingerleaf rodgersia (*R. aesculifolia*)
- Meadowrue (*Thalictrum delavayi* 'Album')

GROUNDCOVERS
- Bugleweed (*Ajuga reptans* 'Bronze Beauty').
- Irish moss (*Sagina subulata*) and Scotch moss (*S. subulata* 'Aurea')
- *Thymus* spp.

Can't believe there was room for 83 plants." The next spring I squeezed in a few more.

The waist-high fence, centred with a gate and arch, was the project's finishing touch. The contractor recommended cedar rather than cheaper pressure-treated lumber because it weathers to an attractive, soft grey. The trellis was custom-made, giving the fence a neat, finished look on both sides, and the gate was made with boards, rather than trellis, for durability.

Well, the final tally—including design consultation, sod removal, construction of the patio, fence and gate, and trees and other plants—exceeded the $3,000 budget, but I'd rather not reveal by precisely how much. (In marriages where only one spouse is a gardener, it's best if the non-gardening spouse does not know how many visits were made to the local nursery.) I saved by starting a few plants from seed, and some were moved from other parts of my garden or given to me by friends.

Even I was surprised at how established the new garden looked the following year, thanks to its protected site, a kind winter and improved soil. The flagstones had already acquired an aged patina, and the cedar fence had begun to weather. I felt a thrill each time I walked around the back corner of the house and caught a glimpse of the tapestry of green and burgundy through the arched gate. Holly still considers it off-limits, and visitors continue to gravitate to it on hot, summer days. ∎

Even a year later the new garden looked established. The flagstones were acquiring the patina of age, and the cedar fence was beginning to weather. Perennial plants, including the hostas and Joe-Pye weed seen at rear, right, and northern sea oats, right foreground, have settled in. Flowering plants, like the annual cleome in left foreground, are kept to white, pink or purple. The garden is off-limits to Holly, but she's allowed in for a photo.

Pam Williams describes a few of the tricks she used to make her garden appear wider and larger than it really is. Pretend you're standing in her morning room, looking north, with the entire garden within your view. Here's what she'd say:

"I tried to create the illusion of depth by planting a round boxwood on the second level that's larger than two round ones on the third level. I'm assuming that objects in the distance look smaller, and by making them smaller still, I enhance the effect."

"The urn in the round area of the second level is definitely a focal point. The flagstones around it are interplanted with blue and white creeping veronicas, which tolerate a half-day of shade and take a good amount of foot traffic."

"The two large cedars in the back soften a tall hard corner and hide the flaking cement on a city wall. They also hide a compost heap."

"The smoke tree contrasts with the white wall. I prune it so it lies flat against the wall and grows upward, not outward, so it doesn't shade the bed in front."

"The large juniper covers an ugly corner where the retaining wall meets the concrete patio. By enlarging the front elements, I also enhance the illusion of depth. It also looks great when it's covered with snow."

"Evergreens add winter interest and create strong architectural lines. The pyramidal yew grows slowly, is hardy and nicely shaped, and it tolerates the shade from my neighbour's large pine."

"The only tall plants I grow are against the side and back walls, and along the left side of the garden. The variegated weigela is pruned like an umbrella so I can see under it to the third level."

"The curving beds take advantage of the sunniest part of the garden and provide extra planting areas that can be seen from the house. The serpentine path echoes the curving beds and softens the linear nature of the garden."

"Two dwarf Alberta spruce flank the steps to create a sense of entry and direct the eye down the major sightline. They've started to get too big for their britches, so I plan to replace them with boxwood clipped to the same shape."

asharedgarden

TWO WINNIPEG GARDENERS DOUBLE THEIR PLEASURE BY EVA WEIDMAN

Marilyn Craggs, left, and Val Perry, next-door neighbours with tiny backyards, turned their small barren backyard into one floriferous garden. The first step was to take down the chain-link fence separating their properties. The next step was a landscaping course.

If laughter makes plants happy, then Val Perry and Marilyn Craggs have an exceptionally joyful garden. Make that two gardens—the women live next door to each other and have turned their two tiny properties into one floriferous, comfortable garden.

When Marilyn, an interior designer, moved back into the old family home she'd grown up in, the backyard did not look hopeful. Nor did the house—so she decided to renovate it. "Soon the backyard was filled with ripped-out lumber, plaster, nails, and glass. It was a disas-

ter," she says. Next door, Val's yard was mostly overgrown grass. "There was a chain-link fence and two sidewalks between the yards. Taking the fence down was the first step toward making them into a garden."

The next step was a landscaping course. Soon the shared garden was underway: the plan included many old-fashioned favourites in a pink/purple/white/yellow scheme. Only one spot of orange was allowed—a huge tiger lily (*Lily tigrinum*) planted by Marilyn's mother more than a decade ago.

Marilyn and Val say sharing the garden is fun, and they learn from each other's mistakes and successes. They're careful to give each other privacy if one of them has company, or when they sense the other just wants to be alone. But when it's time to revel in a new bloom or another botanical reward, they're happy to celebrate together. ∎

Their new garden is anchored with patios of rosy pavers laid in half-circle patterns. From the sidewalks beside each house throughout the back garden, no grass exists. Beds are a bountiful blend of many perennials and annuals, including foxgloves (*Digitalis* spp.), lamb's-ears (*Stachys byzantina*), false sunflowers (*Heliopsis* spp.), morning glories (*Ipomoea* spp.), fuchsias, white and pink phlox, daisies (*Leucanthemum* spp.), sweet peas (*Lathyrus odoratus*) and herbs.

reclaiming theparkinglot

AN ASPHALT DESERT BECOMES A SUNNY ROSE GARDEN   BY CHRISTINE DIRKS

Old mattresses, soggy sofas and garbage once inhabited this London garden, formerly a vehicle-storage area beside a repair depot. Asphalt and greasy dirt were removed and replaced with humus-rich soil and gravel. The enclosed area provides a perfect microclimate for sun-loving plants.

Ann and David Lindsay like old buildings and their surroundings, so it seems natural they would turn the bleak and neglected parking space around their cookware store in London, Ontario, into a court-yard and rose garden. The Lindsays bought the vacant and derelict building that now houses Ann McColl's Kitchen Shop, as well as two interior design shops and artists' studios, in 1984. Then, it was a yellow-brick, three-storey structure built in 1890 as a Massey-Harris tractor showroom and repair depot. The Lindsays decided to renovate the building rather than tear it down, but once that was done, they had to address the 27-square-metre parking space at the south side of the building, adjacent to the shop's large bright kitchen. The area had been a holding area for vehicles awaiting repairs at the farm equipment business.

The view from the shop's doors was harsh, says Ann. "There was graffiti on the wall, broken asphalt, old mattresses, soggy sofas and garbage." They tidied up the area and covered the asphalt with a load of gravel, which was fine for a few years. But in 1992 Ann attended a talk about roses. "I started thinking about adding old-fashioned roses to our garden at home, but there was little room to expand," she says.

There was, however, the recently reclaimed space at the shop. Protected from wind by

discoveryour gardenroom

Though few homes are blessed with a century-old brick wall and the sheltered south-facing space the Lindsays enjoy at their shop in London, Ontario, sizing up what you do have with a critical eye can be useful.

• Look for unused pockets of space. For example, the area adjacent to your garage's rear wall might be underused because it's not visible from the house. That privacy can be its strength. Lattice panels affixed to the garage wall can provide structure for climbing plants and visual texture. If the garage has a window, add a colourful window box. By removing the grass and creating a floor of gravel or flagstone, and adding a garden bench, you've got the basics of a small garden room.

• If the space you're considering is covered in asphalt and the removal cost is prohibitive, consider laying gravel on top, as the Lindsays did, for a more attractive look.

• Think small. The Lindsays' courtyard garden is only 27 square metres. Even a smaller space would accommodate a table, chairs and a few large containers of colourful plants.

• If time and money are in short supply, complete the project over a few years. Create the flowerbeds the first year, and add a small tree and other elements in subsequent years.

the building and by a neighbouring brick wall graced with trumpet vine and grapevine and anchored with a mature raspberry bush, the area's garden potential became clear. "As soon as we visualized roses growing in the sheltered spot by the store, the idea took on a life of its own," Ann says.

Having heard that roses don't like tar, and given that the ground was imbued with it as well as grease, Ann and David removed the asphalt where they planned to create the rose beds, digging down 1 to 1.5 metres. They put in lots of compost, manure and new soil. Instead of planting untried roses, however, they decided to move the hardy and disease-resistant varieties from their home to the shop's courtyard. That made space in their home garden, which had more favourable growing conditions, for the new varieties Ann wanted to try. "We trusted the roses would survive the move. We knew the conditions in the

new garden were likely negative, but the idea of seeing the space become a courtyard quieted any doubts." The roses were moved in the spring and their tops pruned—not many roots were lost in the process, she says.

The Lindsays hired Mike Williams, then just starting out in his landscape business, to help execute their plan. Mike spent a hot Saturday in May removing asphalt and old soil for the beds that would frame the courtyard. After the soil in the beds was amended, the roses were moved into place and underplanted with oregano, marjoram and various thymes.

From spring through fall the enclosed courtyard is a favourite sitting spot for Ann and David Lindsay and the employees of their kitchen shop. The couple moved roses from their home garden and bought some new ones—hybrid teas, climbers and shrub roses in shades from cream to crimson.

One bed was edged with lavender and kept well watered the first season. To finish off the courtyard, the Lindsays added large clay pots planted with a lemon tree, a hibiscus and a bay tree, which they winter indoors, and ivy geraniums. As well as adding colour and texture, the pots emphasize the relaxed mood of the new courtyard.

The 18 moved specimens, along with some new roses—hybrid teas, climbers and shrubs in creamy white, soft pink, deep red, crimson and golden yellow—more than survived. They thrived in their new sunny, sheltered environment. The lively mix of colours was never planned, says Ann, who had purchased most of the plants over several years from grocery stores and a nursery, choosing whatever caught her eye.

When Ann and David began the garden, they decided not to spray or fuss over the plants. "We know roses can be prey to mould, blackspot and pests, but this is a busy shop and there isn't a lot of spare time. We treat blackspot by removing fallen leaves and cutting off affected leaves as soon as we notice them. It's very low maintenance."

They've been pleasantly surprised with the results. " We haven't lost one plant and we often have a second blooming in September." Ann believes that taking chances with roses has its own rewards. "A love of the flower overcomes your fear of problems."

Ann calls the sunny courtyard a release valve. From spring through fall it's a favourite spot for Ann and David and for shop employees, visiting sales representatives and people attending cooking classes. "We often eat lunch here, and it's a delightful place to chat with someone over a pot of tea." The garden is such an established part of the business, Ann can't imagine one without the other. ■

rough and ready roses

Roses have a reputation for being finicky and fickle, relentless in their demands on busy gardeners. "Grow roses?" we say. "No way. My garden's too cold/shady/windy/crowded. And plus my soil is hopeless. Besides, who wants to fuss with all that spraying?"

It's time to compost these misconceptions. The secret is to choose the right rose for your conditions. If you live in Zone 6 or colder, you'll have to give hybrid teas winter protection, or grow them as annuals but, thanks to recent breeding and an increased availability of old, hardy shrub roses, there isn't a garden in Canada that can't support a rose variety or two—or more. Here are some tips for growing roses in less than ideal circumstances.

Too cold: Look no further than the dozens of roses bred in Canada in the past decade or two. The Explorer series includes shrubs and climbers in white and all shades of pink, rose and red. They suffer little, if any, winterkill, bloom from early summer to fall, and most are resistant to blackspot and mildew. Another Canadian series is Parkland, developed in Morden, Manitoba, and bred for Prairie conditions. They're loaded with double and semi-double flowers. If yellow is your colour, look for 'Agnes', a light lemony shade, or the thornless, 'J. P. Connell'. Other shrub roses with iron-clad constitutions are 'Blanc Double de Coubert', 'Celestial', 'Hansa', 'Reine des Violettes' and 'Stanwell Perpetual'.

Too shady: Roses prefer lots of sun, but some varieties tolerate partial shade. 'Charles de Mills', 'The Hunter', 'Mme Hardy', 'Schneezwerg', 'Frau Dagmar Hartopp', the Rosa Mundi rose, and most rugosa roses bloom with just a half-day of sun.

Too windy: Nothing's tougher than a rugosa rose. Wind won't tatter its leathery, crinkly leaves, and its prolific semi-double blooms are sturdy, too. These shrubs also tolerate salt spray, which means they're ideal for seaside settings. Cultivars include 'Blanc Double de Coubert' and 'F. J. Grootendorst'.

Too little space: When most people think of hardy roses, big, arching, spreading shrubs often come to mind. But 'Charles Albanel', 'Henry Hudson', 'Winnipeg Parks' and 'Morden Amorette' all keep to 60 centimetres. Other low growers are Pavement roses, rugosa hybrids from Germany. They're fragrant, steady rebloomers regardless of heat, drought or poor soil. Colours range from white ('Snow Pavement') to purplish-red ('Purple Pavement') with shades of pink and rose in between.

Trellises, obelisks or arbours make use of vertical space in the garden. Climbing Explorers include 'Captain Samuel Holland', 'Henry Kelsey', 'John Cabot' and 'William Baffin'. 'John Davis' has the bonus of being nearly thornless. Others: 'Alchymist' and 'The Polar Star'.

Poor soil: It's a mistake to think roses are particularly demanding. Well-drained soil with plenty of humus is important. Clay soil usually contains more nutrients than sandy soil, and retains nutrients better. Just make sure it's not compacted. Feed all roses monthly once growth starts in spring until a month before fall frosts are expected. Stop deadheading roses at this time so rosehips can form, triggering plants to go dormant.
— Beckie Fox

adrivewayreborn

A UTILITARIAN AREA TURNS INTO A COLOURFUL RETREAT
BY PAUL MARSHMAN

The tiny space, which had been grassed over before it eventually became a garden, is deceiving in its spaciousness. The secret is the design: a diamond-shaped pathway that leads around a birdbath in a centre clearing and a limited colour scheme of flowers planted with a layered effect.

Patti Spencer's garden is living proof that a small space can have a powerful impact. The sheltered side garden, hidden away behind a natural wood fence, is not even visible from the quiet street where Patti and her husband, John, live in Fort Erie, Ontario. Behind the 70-year-old house, however, a wooden arbour hung with vivid blue morning-glories opens a door into a private world of colour and beauty that makes you feel peaceful and relaxed the moment you step into it.

The space, which lived lives as a driveway and a lawn before it became a garden, is 8 metres by 4 metres. But the impression it gives is of a full-size English garden bursting with shapes, colours and textures. Clumps of iris greet you as you enter, flanked by tall heads of white phlox. Purple coneflowers (*Echinacea purpurea*) nod their heads beside long shafts of spider flowers (*Cleome hasslerana*). Cosmos and shasta daisies show their faces from the far end.

Two rose-of-Sharon (*Hibiscus syriacus*), one with white blossoms, the other mauve, provide a backdrop for a bed against the side wall of the house, where fancy pink poppies and hollyhocks thrive in the warm afternoon sunlight. Nearby, 'Heritage', a David Austin rose, sends out its first flowers.

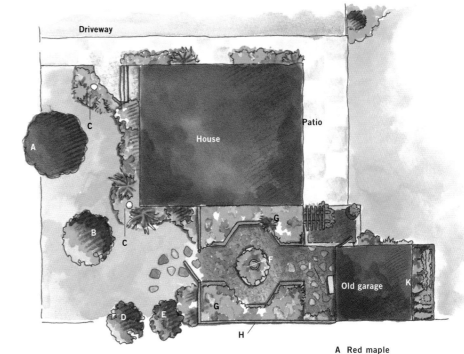

A Red maple
B Flowering almond
C Light standard
D Burning bush
E Lilac
F Birdbath
G Perennials
H Picket fence
I Bench
J Wisteria
K Vegetables

(30 x 18 metres)

Here and there, herbs add green tones—garlic chives in one corner, rosemary and fern-leaf tansy (*Tanacetum vulgare* var. *crispum*) in the other. Thyme (*Thymus* spp.) grows between the fieldstones on the pathway between the beds. Lavender and catmint (*Nepeta* x *faassenii*) peek out from the beds and, farther down, the grey leaves of lamb's-ears (*Stachys byzantina*) add a muted note.

The garden is a tapestry of colours woven in soft shades of pink, blue and white. No strong reds or yellows disrupt the tranquil scene. Intense pink begonias, planted in the tops of clay strawberry jars, brighten the garden at one end, while daylilies (*Hemerocallis* spp.) add pastel tones on both sides of the path: creamy pink on one, a deep cranberry on the other. A snowy carpet of white sweet alyssum (*Lobularia maritima*) throughout the garden sets off the scene.

If it looks like a quiet country retreat, it's no accident. That's what Patti had in mind when she and John set out to create the garden: a place where she could recharge her batteries after long shifts working as an emergency ward nurse at a local hospital. "I don't consider this work," she says, pulling a few errant weeds out of the thickly planted beds. "Work causes stress. This relieves it."

Making a garden, even a small one, from scratch, however, does require work. The

project started with a desire to make use of a section of lawn at the side of the house that had been cut off from the backyard patio by a privacy fence. "I explained to John that if he took down the fence, we could use that area for a lovely little herb garden," says Patti. That was in April, 1994, and by May 24 she was planting.

The challenge was to make the garden look full while at the same time creating a feeling of spaciousness. The solution was a central design—a fieldstone pathway leading to a diamond-shaped clearing in the middle of the area and a birdbath as its central focus. "We made the path wide enough for a wheelbarrow," says Patti. "I knew I wanted something in the centre, and I had to have access so I could get in with compost, rocks, and plants."

The picket fence surrounding the garden was planned just as meticulously, built high at one end for privacy and sloped down to the other end, where a gate opens into the front yard. Like the garden, the fence is handmade. "John built the fence, and cut every little picket," says Patti proudly.

Since the area was a driveway before becoming a patch of lawn, Patti decided to

savingwater

With so many plants in a small space soaking up lots of water during hot summers, Patti Spencer needed a plan, especially when Fort Erie began metering water several years ago. Thanks to a little ingenuity, the garden needs almost no municipal water, relying mostly on what's collected by Patti and John.

"We stuck an old wooden rain barrel under the downspout, but put a plastic garbage can inside to catch the rain because the barrel leaks," Patti says. "And the central air-conditioning was forever backing up, so we put a big bucket under the outlet. To water the plants, I dip a can into one of these containers—I very rarely need to turn the hose on."

The garden is also easy on water because of its design and the way it's planted. The beds are mostly compost, which retains water well, and they're mulched with leaves and wood chips so little soil surface is exposed to wind and sun.

dig in compost and raise the beds. "We didn't know if the driveway had been paved or not and, even if not, the soil would be compacted—not great for plants." The beds are edged with mini railway ties and filled with earth and compost, obtained free from Fort Erie's municipal composting program.

In fact, the garden is a blending of many contributions and found objects. John, Patti, and Patti's daughter Erin, 14 years old at the time, hunted through favourite spots on the nearby Niagara Escarpment for flat stones to make the pathway, and friends, neighbours and relatives contributed a large number of the plants. The David Austin rose had been a wedding gift three years earlier, the goutweed (*Aegopodium podagraria* 'Variegatum') came from John's mother, and poppies were a contribution from a co-worker.

The garden is a tiny encyclopedia of plants, but Patti imposes a sense of order, repeating colours and species for harmonious effect. The tallest plants, blue and white delphiniums, are the same height as the fence, and Patti removes the lower branches of the rose-of-Sharon shrubs— original occupants of the site—so flowers can be planted at their base. The result is a layered garden that's full and lush, yet not overgrown.

While she didn't design her garden after any formal model, Patti sees her own character and heritage reflected in it. "When I look at pictures of English gardens, I recognize mine," she says. "My mother's family came from England. Somewhere in the family tree there had to have been a gardener."

Her family, however, has its own name for the garden: the Big Thyme Garden. "John kept saying, 'You're going to owe me big time for all this work,'" says Patti, "so Erin started calling it the Big Time Garden. Later, when I planted thyme as a groundcover, we just changed the spelling." ∎

treesfor smallspaces

Plenty of trees are suitable for small lots and do not outgrow their space nor require expensive tree surgery to keep them under control. Here are some favourites of Trevor Cole, former director of the National Arboretum in Ottawa.

Small enough for a pocket-handkerchief garden and a thriving grower even in poor, sandy soils, 'Walker' Siberian peashrub (*Caragana arborescens* 'Walker', Zone 2) forms

a narrow column about 1 metre wide and 2 metres tall at maturity. It has a weeping habit and its small, almost thread-like, leaves are pale green. In late May the tree is clothed in bright yellow flowers resembling small sweet peas. The winter silhouette is attractive and its rounded top makes a good perch for birds. Japanese maple (*Acer palmatum*, Zone 6) is sold in many named forms with beautifully coloured and dissected leaves. Trees should be planted in rich soil; protect from wind and late-spring frost. Japanese maples grow from 3 metres by 4 metres up to

The whitewashe...
sits at the lot lir...
climbing roses...
house. The wa...
warmth. Below...

grass gradua...
individual b...
Pam's reduc...

She cuts...
with barely...
mower and...
tuning with...
makes the...
once again...
false clues.
Pam prom...
the rest of...
colour to...
and flower...

Keeping...
challenge...
somethin...
as if I'm...
Pam says...
the rise to...
planting...
don't gro...

Pam a...
gardenin...
persona...
dwarf pl...
would s...
scale by...
a lot m...
she say...
Wonde...
ger as t...

After you have taken in the feast of colours and textures in the foreground, the cunning design draws your eye to the sides of the garden and toward the top level, where huge hostas and tall ferns grow. Pam puts brightly coloured plants on the lowest level to draw attention.

front
entra
below
tarpa
backy
seem
walls
3 me
the s
next
Pam
was
four
  I
with
step
ly b
viev
face
the
in
rol
hu
to
de
th
de
u
th
a
tc
d
p
p
d
t
l
c
l
c

buildingabog

It took Pam Williams close to two weeks of back-breaking work to install a two-level pond with just the right sound of trickling water at the end of her backyard. It took about two minutes for her to realize she couldn't hear it from the patio. Then she forgot to turn the pump off one night, and the motor burned out.

Frustrated, Pam left it as a still pond. Then the mosquitoes started to breed. Knowing she had to remove the water from the pond, yet dreading the idea of ripping out the heavy liner, she came up with an idea. If she could get the water to drain slowly, but never completely, she could turn it into a bog garden.

On the advice of a friend, Pam cut several drainage holes in the liner along the bottom and sides of the pond, about 30 centimetres from ground level. She covered the bottom with a layer of gravel and filled the empty pond with a combination of approximately three parts topsoil to one part peat moss. She keeps her bog garden damp at all times, watering by hand if rainfall is insufficient.

If you want a bog garden without the expense or trouble of installing a heavy liner, make it from green garbage bags. First, choose the site carefully. Since water retention is the point of a bog, find a spot that doesn't get too much sun or the soil may dry out. Dig a hole about 15 centimetres deep. Take one or two garbage bags; slit one side and the bottom of each so the bags will lie flat, and place them over the bottom and sides of the excavation. Puncture the plastic in a few places, layer the bottom with gravel and fill with a peaty soil mixture.

Water the bog frequently, making sure it stays wet all summer.

This back part of the garden, the last terrace of the three rising from the house, has a completely different feeling. Ferns grow high here, and huge hostas look tropical—there's a sense that the garden is stretching its legs. Two bog gardens, where a two-level trickling pond once briefly burbled, are rich with peat and moisture-loving marsh plantings, including astilbe, campanula and primula. If you turn around here to look back at the lower levels of the garden, everything seems to look different; the height, the perspective, and the light combine to invite the visitor to return and rediscover the garden.

This illusion is created in part by Pam's choices of foliage, which seem to change with the light and the height from which they are viewed. But her judgment was not always so effective. "I'm a sucker for two things—variegated leaves and lacy, frothy foliage," she says. "But by using too many I made the garden look blurry." So she realized it was time to learn about contrast, and began a concerted effort to find plants with strongly defined foliage that look good on their own and enhance the leaves and flowers of their neighbours. She sharpened the soft and fuzzy look by adding compact leaves with jagged edges. She looks for tall spiky flowering plants like blazing star (*Liatris punctata, L. spicata*) and anything—absolutely anything—that creeps, such as varieties of veronica, sedum, aubrieta and campanula.

Having faced her challenges of height and foliage, Pam next wanted to experiment with colour. She decided to plant different colours of flowers together, "to dare nature to make a mistake." Her conclusion: "It's almost impossible to get a bad match."

Not all of her trials are successful, though. Following another principle of perspective to create a sense of distance, she planted bright colours in the foreground and paler ones in the distance. "But the pale colours in the background just got lost," she admits. Now she puts bright colours in the back to catch attention.

And attention is what this garden demands, all year long. Fern-leafed bleeding heart (*Dicentra formosa* 'Luxuriant') blooms from spring to August; medium and larger iris bring in the summer solstice. There are roses ('Alexander MacKenzie', an Explorer rose, and 'Carefree Beauty'), pasqueflower, salvia and aubrieta. Pam plants rue for its blue-green foliage and purple coneflowers for late-summer colour. A clutch of shasta daisies offers a month of colour, while the soft, woolly leaves of lamb's-ears (*Stachys byzantina*) are spread throughout the beds. In winter the focus changes: the garden's evergreens supplemented with others in planters placed strategically on the three terraces give the garden strong architectural lines. The dried leaves and stems of large sedums and miniature astilbes poking through the snow add more interest.

Perhaps Pam's greatest achievement in her small garden has been to create the illusion of simplicity and balance: with all its complexity, the garden looks right. And as she continues to work at mastering the challenges of a small space, Pam dreams of gardening on a grand scale. "I was thinking Sissinghurst Castle," she jokes. In the meantime, she'll continue with the conjuring tricks that make her tiny yard such an amazing and enjoyable spectacle. ■

theartofillusion

SUBTLE GRADE CHANGES AND CLEVER PRUNING TRANSFORM A GARDEN
BY PATRICIA MAITLAND

To suggest width, Pam Williams used horizontal lines—wide steps and flat stones—and keeps tall plants at the sides so they don't block the view. The upward-sloping garden is terraced in three shallow levels, and the middle level is dominated by a Grecian urn, the focal point. Above: balloon flower

Be warned when you walk into Pam Williams' home: she's trying to trick you. See the window with a beautiful view of cascading wisteria? Look again—it's not real; it's a wall painting created by Pam. And the bookshelf over there, with a collection of leather-bound classics? Another trompe l'oeil created out of Pam's passion for whimsy. So when a glance toward the back of the house reveals a formal garden stretching up and away from a grand picture window, you're quick to assume it's just another illusion.

In fact, it's the real thing. You can stand in it, stroll in it, peek and peer and sniff—do all the wonderful things a garden invites you to do. But Pam has applied the same techniques an artist uses to create the sense of a large, expansive garden on a small, narrow lot. Instead of paints and brushstrokes, she's used plants and shallow terraces, which have also helped solve the problem of the original sloping lot.

Walking with Pam in her garden in the Riverdale area of Toronto, one realizes that Pam and her plants have a symbiotic relationship. As she took on the challenge of turning this former wasteland into a garden, this little piece of land managed to turn Pam Williams into a gardener.

When she moved into her house in 1982, the narrow yard in the back was completely uninviting. The lot sloped upward from the

agardenoffice

A WINNIPEG REAL—ESTATE AGENT MAKES WORKING AT HOME FUN
BY EVA WEIDMAN

Terie Langen mixes business with pleasure by starting her morning with coffee and a stroll through her pretty garden as she mulls over the day's activities. Her garden is often inspiration for clients looking for potential in small spaces.

Terie Langen's clients get an unexpected bonus when she takes them on inspection tours of homes for sale in her sales territory. Once the pictures of the grandchildren have been shown, she pulls pictures of her garden from her wallet.

Terie's tiny Winnipeg garden is not just integral to her personal life—it has become an extension of her office. As a home-based real estate agent, she has the pleasure of starting her day with a cup of coffee and a stroll through her garden, from herb bed to vegetable patch to flower border. There's always a new gift to greet her, a fresh flower bud or a suddenly ripe, pink tomato.

Terie complements the lady's-mantle (*Alchemilla mollis*), petunias, raspberries and grapevines in her garden with furniture and accessories. "I look at the garden as another room of my house, so I set it up with pieces that have meaning for me," she says.

Candles, torches, wind chimes and ceramics are tucked among the basil, parsley, roses, Russian sage (*Perovskia atriplicifolia*), phlox and lilies in her eclectic mix of edible and decorative plants.

Terie says mixing business with pleasure is perfect for her because her clients are often interested in the gardening potential of a property they're considering. "And if they think a yard is too small to do much with, I have my pictures ready," she laughs. ▪

Above and left are two
small trees eminently
suitable for small
gardens; each has
different attributes. The
Japanese maple, above,
has fabulous coloured
foliage, interesting form
and is a slow grower.
Siberian peashrub can
grow in contorted
shapes, like the old
one at left, and is
covered with yellow
flowers in May.

5 metres by 6 metres, depending on cultivar.

Weeping white mulberry (*Morus alba* 'Pendula', Zone 4) has a pleasing umbrella shape that provides young children with a wonderful hiding place. It grows to about 2 metres wide and 2.5 metres tall. The small raspberry-like fruit is edible (birds love it) but stains clothing and sidewalks.

Pagoda dogwood (*Cornus alternifolia*, Zone 3b) is a small, native tree that prefers acidic soil in light shade; however, it grows well in slightly alkaline soil and full sun in Trevor Cole's garden. (It gets its common name from the branch tips, which turn up- ward slightly.) In late spring, clusters of white flowers are held just above the almost horizontal branches. By late summer, the green fruit turns to red and almost black; clouds of birds can strip the tree bare in a couple of days. Grows to 6 metres tall and is 7.5 metres wide at maturity, which takes

This page: flowering dogwood is a beautiful small tree and comes in several cultivars. Opposite, top row: double-flowering pink almond, sold either as a shrub (as here) or as a tree grafted onto a stem; and the tiny Sargent crabapple, which has good disease resistance and thrives in most soils. Bottom row: 'Fastigiata' columnar English oak; and golden chain tree, which has gorgeous yellow blooms with a wisteria-like form.

more than 30 years. The flowering and kousa dogwoods (*C. florida*, and *C. kousa*) grow well to Zone 7 and Zone 6, respec- tively. Both have showy spring flowers (really bracts), good fall colour and edible red fruit. Alternative choices of flowering dogwoods include 'Rubra', with pink flowers, and 'First Lady', with variegated yellow-green foliage, and both prefer acidic soil in full sun. They can be prone to pests (dogwood borer and leaf miner) and diseases (anthracnose and powdery mildew). Both form trees about 6 metres tall and wide.

Sargent crabapple (*Malus sargentii*, Zone 5) is a tiny tree that grows less than 2 metres tall and 3 metres wide, has good disease resistance and thrives in most soils, making it better than others of its species for small gardens. In spring, red buds open into white flowers, which give rise to small, bright red fruit. 'Tina' is said to be an even smaller cultivar and is worth searching for. The upright Siberian crab (*M. baccata* 'Columnaris', Zone 2) forms a narrow column about 9 metres tall by 1.5 metres wide. It prefers a medium soil and at least a half-day of sun. The white flowers are followed by small red or yellow fruits.

plant solutions

The striking golden chain (*Laburnum* x *watereri* 'Vossii', Zone 6) has pendulous flower chains up to 45 centimetres long in spring. Grow in well-drained soil in full sun, in a spot where the olive-green bark can be appreciated from indoors in winter. Reaches about 4.5 metres by 3.5 metres, and can be trained over a pergola. On the downside, the seeds are poisonous, so avoid planting close to a sidewalk where children might pick them up.

Double-flowering almond (*Prunus triloba* 'Multiplex', Zone 2b) is sold as either a shrub or a tree. The tree form (usually sold as 'Plena') is grafted onto a stem and makes a good small tree about 5 metres tall by 3 metres wide. The spring flowers are tiny pink cotton balls that clothe the branches so thickly they almost hide the leaves.

'Schubert' chokecherry, also known as 'Canada Red' (*Prunus virginiana* 'Schubert', Zone 2) has a rounded head that grows about 7 metres tall and 6 metres wide, but it takes 30 years. Green foliage darkens to dull purple, and the white spring flowers give purple fruit that's good for preserves if lots of sugar is added.

Many conifers add height and winter in-terest to a small garden. Conical forms include dwarf Alberta spruce (*Picea glauca* var. *albertiana* 'Conica', Zone 4) and several cultivars of white cedar (*Thuja occidentalis*, Zone 3), including bright green 'Holmstrup' and 'Reingold', with golden foliage that turns coppery in winter. The Alberta spruce reaches 3 metres, the others 2 metres, again in about 30 years. Columnar shapes include dwarf Serbian spruce (*P. omorika* 'Nana', Zone 2b), upright white cedars such as *T. o.* 'Fastigiata' and 'Unicorn', and

numerous narrow forms of juniper, such as *Juniperus chinensis* 'Fairview' (Zone 5), *J. scopulorum* 'Skyrocket' (Zone 3) and *J. virginiana* 'Manhattan Blue' (Zone 2b). These all grow 3 metres to 5 metres tall and are suitable for most soils.

Lawson's false cypress (*Chamaecyparis lawsoniana*, Zone 6), comes in several narrow, upright selections, including some that are quite miniature. Selections grow 3 metres to 15 metres tall by 1 metre to 3 metres wide.

Columnar English oak (*Quercus robur* 'Fastigiata', Zone 4) is a deciduous tree with glossy, dark green leaves. It's slow-growing to 15 metres but only 4 metres wide. ▪

Kousa dogwood, above, has showy spring bracts that look like flowers, good fall colour, edible fruit and is hardy to Zone 6. Other selections will grow in colder climates. Opposite: Lawson's false cypress is a stately evergreen of elegant appearance with cultivars that grow only to 3 metres tall.

sideyard savvy

Long, narrow sideyards are too often neglected. Most people cover them with a layer of gravel or just leave it as grass, soon trampled from repeated foot traffic. But these difficult areas can become a verdant jewel in a gardener's crown.

The owners of the neglected sideyard here, a sparsely planted passage 6.3 metres long by 1.35 metres wide at the gate, narrowing to 1.65 metres at the garden end, decided to renovate.

Plant life consisted of invasive variegated goutweed (*Aegopodium podagraria* 'Variegatum'), ho-hum violets (*Viola* spp.), golden creeping Jenny (*Lysimachia nummularia* 'Aurea') and a young upright cedar near the deck, all of which did fine in the limited sunlight (three hours at midday, under Zone 5 conditions). Red crushed brick formed a partial path that allowed runoff to percolate into the soil, but it perversely stopped midway down the narrow space.

The pathway from the front yard to the side door of this house (seen before its renovation, opposite), had been treated to a few plants and a crushed-brick surface, but it was in need of a lift. The redesign was simple: a few strategically placed patio stones that zigzag slightly to carry the eye to the plantings and decorative rocks, and plants chosen for variety in leaf shape, colour and height.

practical solutions

Ivy

Dwarf goatsbeard

To make the path more appealing and connect with the deck's steps, rectangular grey patio stones were combined with red ones 30 centimetres square, creating a checkerboard pattern with a strong graphic element. To break up what could have been a long, too-straight path, it was zigzagged toward the fence, then toward the deck, leaving planting pockets on both sides. Crushed brick was added to stabilize the stones and facilitated drainage.

Only the creeping Jenny and the dwarf pyramidal cedar (*Thuja occidentalis* 'Holmstrup') were kept. Weeds and grass were removed, and soil in the planting pockets was cultivated and amended with triple mix.

To break up the fence line, a chocolate vine (*Akebia quinata*) was planted halfway down the space and an upright 'Hill's' yew softens the jog where the storage bench beside the house meets the deck. The chocolate vine climbs thin wires stretched between eyehooks screwed into the fence—a simple way to create an unobtrusive trellis.

A few large rocks were grouped on either side of the path to add visual interest, and a small glazed birdbath brightens the area.

Shade-tolerant perennial groundcovers with interesting leaf shapes and textures were chosen: glossy, bold bergenia (*Bergenia cordifolia* 'Baby Doll') and bugleweed (*Ajuga reptans* 'Bronze Beauty') contrast with ferns, feathery sea oats (*Chasmanthium latifolium*) and lacy dwarf goatsbeard (*Aruncus aethusifolius*). Golden-leafed buttercup (*Ranunculus repens* 'Buttered Popcorn') ties in with the yellow creeping Jenny.

A mulch of shredded cedar bark over exposed soil was the finishing touch, to reduce evaporation and discourage weeds. It also helps keep soil in place when rainwater runs down the slope. ■

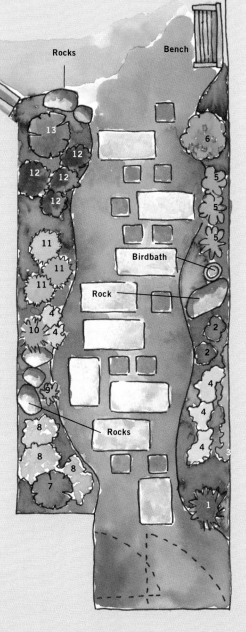

1 Christmas fern
   (*Polystichum acrostichoides*, Zone 4)
2 'Brokamp' English ivy
   (*Hedera helix* 'Brokamp', Zone 7)
3 Chocolate vine
   (*Akebia quinata*, Zone 5)
4 Golden creeping Jenny
   (*Lysimachia nummularia* 'Aurea',
   Zone 3)
5 'Baby Doll' bergenia
   (*Bergenia cordifolia* 'Baby Doll',
   Zone 4)
6 Shrubby cinquefoil
   (*Potentilla fruticose* 'Pink Beauty',
   Zone 3)
7 Hill's yew
   (*Taxus* x *media* 'Hillii', Zone 5)

8 Golden variegated creeping buttercup
   (*Ranunculus repens* 'Buttered
   Popcorn', Zone 3)
9 Hart's-tongue fern
   (*Phyllitis scolopendrium* syn.
   Asplenium scolopendrium
   'Kaye's Lacerate', Zone 4)
10 Northern sea oats
   (*Chasmanthium latifolium*, Zone 5)
11 Dwarf goatsbeard
   (*Aruncus aethusifolius*, Zone 4)
12 'Bronze Beauty' bugleweed
   (*Ajuga reptans* 'Bronze Beauty',
   Zone 3)
13 Dwarf pyramidal cedar
   (*Thuja occidentalis* 'Holmstrup',
   Zone 2)

a oats   Bergenia   Creeping buttercup   Bugleweed

Breaking up the angle of the pathway not only created an eye-pleasing shape, it left good-size pockets for small plants. Because plants in sideyards usually grow in tight quarters, which limits root growth, in shady conditions and neglected soil, compost should be incorporated and the beds should be well mulched to maintain nutrient levels. Use bold foliage, contrasting textures and glossy leaves that reflect light. Small-leafed plants can make a small garden look smaller. Left: chocolate vine was trained on wire to break up the long fence.

mini mirrors

A small mirror can add sparkle and light to tiny sitting areas or reflect light into small basement entranceways, as is often seen in European townhouse gardens. In the photo top right, the combination of mirror and trelliswork softened by vines adds interest to a plain brick wall. The mirror in the garden at lower right fools the eye into thinking it's a window, making the secluded corner even more room-like. Small mirrors can also be set low in garden beds, reflecting plants and giving the impression the planting is larger and more lush. Mirrored gazing balls, with their smooth, shimmering finish, are another way to enhance a small garden. A couple of gazing balls floating in a garden pond reinforce the fluid quality of the play of light on water. A basic rule when placing even small mirrors is to be sure they reflect an attractive tableau, such as a well-shaped tree or an arbour drenched with roses.

Just like larger mirrors, small mirrors that have been permanently installed on walls or fences should be protected with plywood backing sealed and with silicone (see Mirror Basics, page 100, for how-to). But small portable mirrors, unframed or framed, can be used all summer in the garden and brought inside for winter protection. Small mirrors fool the eye—on an old shed one can appear to be a window looking into another part of the garden; set at ground level in a perennial bed a mirror can visually expand a lovely planting.

takecover

When the hot days of summer arrive, gardens—and gardeners—can wilt beneath the scorching sun. A canopy made of a sheet or a table-cloth clipped to poles with curtain rings can save the day. It's quick to make and easy to remove in rain or shade.

For a temporary shelter from the sun, a length of billowy fabric—such as an inexpensive linen tablecloth—makes a pretty canopy.

For the canopy frame, use 2.4-metre bamboo stakes (available at garden centres) about 2.5 centimetres in diameter. You'll need 12 stakes for a free-standing frame, or 7 if the frame is anchored to the wall of a shed or other structure, as is shown here. For extra strength, two stakes are used to support each corner; single stakes are fine for the crosspieces. (Three crosspieces only are used for a canopy attached to a structure.)

Pound the pairs of corner stakes at least 15 centimetres into the ground, spacing them no more than 2.1 metres apart. It's easier if you drive a metal spike into the ground first to make a hole for the bamboo. Consider the length of the fabric when determining the distance between stakes—you'll want a valance to hang down at least 30 centimetres on two of the sides (as shown). For a tight fit, fill extra space in the holes around each stake

with crushed gravel or stones.

Slip four or five curtain rings with clips over two of the crosspieces. With a partner (and standing on a ladder, if necessary), tie the crosspieces to the supporting stakes with wire or rope. Tie at each corner no less than 2.1 metres from the ground.

Clip fabric to rings as desired. Use tent stakes and rope to stabilize the structure. ∎

unique umbrella

Lay the fabric on the cardboard and press flat to secure while painting. Work on one section at a time.

Spray adhesive onto the back of the stencil and press into position on fabric.

Load applicator evenly with paint, removing excess by brushing or rolling onto paper towel until the applicator feels dry.

Build up colour gradually for a crisp outline. Remove and reposition stencil as necessary to repeat the pattern.

Spray the cover with a fabric protector that repels water and dirt and protects against sun damage. Replace cover. ▪

Give an inexpensive umbrella an individual touch with a stencilled design.

Use acrylic craft paints with a stencil brush or foam roller. Remove cover from umbrella frame. Pre-washing is recommended only if you plan to wash the cover after stencilling.

To keep fabric stable for painting, cut a piece of cardboard slightly larger than the size of the stencil and spray one side with stencil adhesive.

It doesn't take a lot of skill to stencil a packaged design (or one of your own making) onto a plain patio umbrella, and an original umbrella gives your garden a unique touch. Or dress up a rain umbrella for an easy and decorative way to protect potted plants too big to move from the unforgiving sun.

whenless ismore

This garden is proof positive that even a space almost literally no bigger than a postage stamp can have appeal beyond the ordinary. The home, a 6-metre by 17-metre structure built in a downtown Toronto alley once filled with weeds and old cars, belongs to architects Brigitte Shim and Howard Sutcliffe. To gain privacy,

the designers wrapped a high stucco wall around the site, and then excavated at one end, sinking the level of open, airy, living/ dining room and the garden below grade. Inside they built upward, creating vertical lines with a fireplace wall and a central stairway topped by a huge skylight.

Adding to the illusion of expansiveness, the living room's mahogany-and-glass end wall pivots open, literally merging the garden with the house. "We started with the notion of the garden as a walled ruin—a lush, romantic, overgrown place," says Howard. The window is multi-functional, serving as frame, wall

and entry point—a transitional element, as a gate might be in a larger landscape. Beyond, the compact garden features a sculptural fountain that is kept running all year to add movement, sound and spirals of steam—or icicles, depending on the season.

A clean-cut pool edged with purply-black clay pavers flashes with six stout koi. Raised beds (planted with rhododendrons, English ivy, a climbing hydrangea and a star magnolia) hug the edges of the patio. Tiny but intense, the meditative garden offers beauty and refreshment: textured greens, snow-etched branches, the purl of water and the fleeting fragrances of rain-washed leaves. ▪

Borrow from traditional models to create elegance and style in your garden

classic gardens

68 NEW WORLD CLASSIC

74 DIVIDE AND CONQUER

80 BORROWED BEAUTY

88 PEACE IN THE CITY

STYLISH SOLUTIONS
94 GOOD GARDEN BONES
98 CLASSIC REFLECTIONS
100 MIRROR BASICS
102 CONTAINER MAGIC

newworldclassic

EUROPE INSPIRES A GARDEN WITH A FRENCH TWIST BY SHIRLEY BLEVINS

The three subtle levels of the Armstrong garden are visible in the view opposite, from the rear of the property. The flagstones, now nicely softened with low plants, give access for maintenance to a bed with dwarf azalea, Siberian iris, Japanese maple, juniper and more, including the mauve clematis at left.

The French have a lot to teach us," says Diana Armstrong, whose nouveau-French townhouse in Toronto's bustling Yonge-Eglinton area boasts a *petit jardin français* in the backyard. "Their formal gardens are geometric, with beautifully scaled proportions, and they excel at focusing the eye on distance."

Diana and her husband, Michael, have spent many vacations in France, where they became inspired by the classic style of the country's formal gardens. They have particu-

larly fond memories of Lucinière, a classic chateau in France's Loire Valley, whose huge garden features expanses of lawn bordered by topiary trees. "But in Lucinière, Mike and I felt a little uncomfortable relaxing like North Americans because we knew we cluttered the landscape—people in shorts, sipping gin and tonics and reading books in lawn chairs tend to spoil the flawless design," says Diana.

So when they moved into their townhouse in the late '90s, their aim was to maintain the integrity of French formal design but make their new garden "people-relaxing and friendly." Before the packing boxes were emptied, Diana took measuring tape and graph paper and designed a formal, geometric garden to suit both the property and their lifestyle. The rear garden was a long, narrow, slanting strip of land 7.5 metres by 45 metres,

formal gardens is evident in twin black urns and metal obelisks entwined with pink mandevilla (*Mandevilla splendens*, a flowering evergreen shrub native to South America) on each side of the trellis, in the shed's windows and window boxes, and in the flanking back fences and the flower boxes. On the lower patio, dual plantings of 'Big Blue' hostas, white coralbells (*Heuchera* spp.) mixed with maidenhair ferns (*Adiantum pedatum*), topiary-style cypress trees and yew trees mirror each other, and two white stone benches bracket an ornamental iron pedestal table holding a white mandevilla spilling from a pot.

Diana's English roots are revealed in the meandering flagstone path along the west side of the garden, the trellis covered with roses and clematis dividing the two expanses of lawn, and the variable, free-form garden near the lawn closest to the garden shed.

There's a hint of French formality in the view from the bottom of the garden toward the house, with the two free-standing wisteria-covered trellises on the patio next to the house, the ornamental-iron fencing and the patio furniture. But the arresting array of potted plants there and throughout the garden is pure Armstrong.

Diana designs, gardens and weeds. Mike maintains the lawn, and prunes with great relish. "We call him Michael Scissorhands," chuckles Diana, a floral designer who creates arrangements from dried, fresh and silk flowers. The couple agrees that Mike's accounting background (he's retired from the investment banking business) could have something to do with his meticulous

with a fence along one side. Several Manitoba maples and a 50-year-old cedar hedge stood across the back. Once the plan was ready, a landscaper removed trees and shrubbery, planted paper-white birches and installed the patios, fencing, brickwork and lawn. Then Diana and Mike took over, creating a relaxed look featuring privacy rather than open spaces.

The south-facing backyard is divided into three levels. From the first level, the large patio next to the house, three steps lead down to a circular brick patio and an expanse of lawn with a large central trellis. The third level, one step down to another

patch of lawn (bordered in stone, in the French manner), leads to a lower brick patio and the garden house. Beds brimming with roses, irises, begonias, phlox, foxglove, poppies, fall anemones, ferns, trillium and astilbe border the lawns.

The view from the upper patio focuses on the garden house, which is framed by the central trellis between the two sections of lawn. The symmetry of French

The interlocking patio nearest the house, at far left, steps down to a small circular seating area where Diana likes to sit. It's framed with formal urns and holds classic iron furniture. The pink foxgloves in the garden near the rear shed, left, and in closeup, opposite, are a favourite plant.

mowing, clipping and pruning skills.

During the growing season, Diana is in the garden every day. "I never admit how many hours I spend there," she says. " I may go out to water the containers [30 or more boxes, planters and urns], but before I'm done, I'm pulling weeds and maybe moving a plant here or there."

Diana pushes the envelope with some plants, such as the wisteria she wasn't sure was hardy in her area. "But it survives—and blooms—because of its southern exposure, protected by the house." She also nurtures azaleas and rhododendrons, pink and yellow lady-slipper orchids, and a standard white rose that she buries every fall and resurrects every spring.

Many of the pots and containers are filled with tropical plants—hibiscus, mandevilla, glorybush (*Tibouchina*), leadwort (*Plumbago* spp.), *Curcuma* (a tropical herb belonging to the ginger family), potato vine (*Solanum jasminoides*), datura (*Brugmansia suaveolens*) and lily-of-the-Nile (*Agapanthus umbellatus*). The

tropicals thrive in the Toronto summer, but must overwinter indoors.

Diana collects multiple varieties of peonies and likes to point out her Japanese tree peonies, along with the red and green Japanese maples, magnolias, yews and a topiary-style blue spruce near the main patio. One of her favourite floral treasures is the pink-flowering dogwood in the upper west corner of the garden. "It just knocks your socks off," she says proudly.

Water fountains add to the garden's sensory appeal. An ivy-covered lion's-head wall fountain hangs on the west fence adjacent to the upper patio, and a miniature water garden in a large, pale blue pot sits on the patio behind the house. It contains a graceful arrangement of water hyacinths, water lettuce and a large, burgundy-leafed taro plant that nods gently to the motion of a small fountain cascading just above the water's surface. "I also included waterlilies," says Diana, "but the raccoons kept pulling them out."

The garden is a magnet for wildlife. "Every morning I have to fill in the squirrel holes," Diana complains. Last year, a

frenchelements

Formal French-château gardens are geometrically and symmetrically designed, and they feature large rectangular sections of grass bordered by stone and clipped trees. Typically, the lawn is bisected with a grand, sweeping driveway lined with equidistant oaks or other large trees. When it comes to flowers, less is often better. Too many clutter the elegant design. The few that adorn a French formal garden are always arranged geometrically.

BRICKWORK
Brickwork is a major element in Diana and Michael Armstrong's garden. The patio near the house is made of interlocking bricks recycled from the front parking pad, which the Armstrongs had redone because it was uneven. The two lower round patios are of similar brick.

COBBLESTONES
To ease the monotony of interlocking brick on the patio nearest the house, the Armstrongs inset a pathway of cobblestones curving from the back door to the stairs leading to the second level. The cobblestones were originally used to secure Toronto streetcar tracks, and the Armstrongs bought a supply several years ago when the city was removing tracks.

FRONTENAC STONE
Weathered, white Frontenac stones from Quebec form a border in the front garden, and about 15 are scattered throughout the back to tie the design together. Frontenac stones also surround the birch trees.

FLAGSTONES
A flagstone path was installed to protect the grass around the garden shed. At first, Diana felt they compromised the overall design. "But once the garden filled in with plants, shrubs and trees, the flagstones began to blend in," she says.

From the house patio,
the formality and
symmetry of the couple's
French-style garden is
apparent. The central
trellis, over which roses
and clematis are being
trained, divides the
garden and marks the
step down to the third
level. Containers burst-
ing with plants are also
an important element
—the two below hold
tender *Streptocarpus*
and violas.

den of foxes lived under the garden shed.
"The cubs chewed through our soaker
hoses and chased birds and squirrels
through the garden, causing a lot of damage," she says. But the birds—cardinals,
eastern blue jays, woodpeckers, hummingbirds—are always a welcome sight.

The cedar garden fencing can't keep
out the local wildlife, but it does offer privacy from neighbours close by. It's softened by many trellises supporting clematis, honeysuckle and roses, and a silver-
lace vine (*Polygonum aubertii*) that gives
the back patio total privacy.

Accents, such as a sundial hidden at
the back adjacent to the flagstone path,
add a stylish touch, and a weather-treated
pine cabinet on the patio near the house
stores small garden tools and doubles as
a buffet table for summer entertaining.

Of course, there are plans to improve
the garden. "We'd like a built-in water
garden and reflecting pool somewhere,"
says Diana, "and we've thought about a
roof garden on the third-storey deck."

What happens when they run out of
room? "If we stay here, we'll always be
trying out new ideas and new plant combinations," Diana says. "On the other
hand, if we move, it will be fun to start a
new garden." She looks thoughtful as she
imagines new horticultural horizons to
conquer. ■

divideand conquer

HAVE A PLAN, SAYS THIS GARDENER, BUT STAY FLEXIBLE   BY ALAIN CHAREST

After a season mulling over design, the author decided to deal with his large garden by dividing it into sections. Behind the house, a carpet of grass bordered with gravel paths and wide perennial beds create a formal garden room, with a trellis hiding a protected dining area. Left: purple *Verbascum phoeniceum*

Starting a garden from scratch with no experience can be rather daunting. Should you start with flower beds? What about putting in shrubs? What kind of shrubs? My own experience designing and redesigning my garden has taught me that enthusiasm is the best asset for guiding you through a process of trial and error.

When I bought my century-old Kitchener, Ontario, house more than 20 years ago, the garden had been abandoned for several years. Except for some diseased plum trees and two pear trees, the yard was filled with goldenrod and purple loosestrife, with a few peonies among them struggling to survive. I took possession in late August, believing I'd lost an entire growing season, but in retrospect I realized the delay was a boon: it forced me to sit down and do some planning. Otherwise, I might have started buying plants and sticking them in anywhere.

By most contemporary urban standards, my back garden, at 21 metres by 58 metres, is rather large. Since there was a willow tree the size of an apartment building in the backyard next door, my first concern was to find the sunniest exposure for a flower bed. I chose to put it along a boundary fence facing southeast, where it could be seen from the house.

I spent the first fall in the backyard clearing out weeds in the area closest to the house. Not having a lot of money for plants,

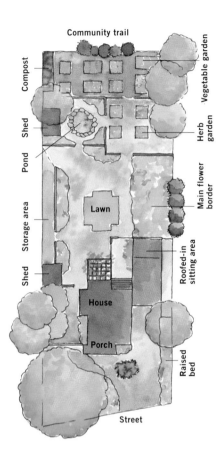

Community trail

Compost

Shed

Pond

Storage area

Shed

Vegetable garden

Herb garden

Main flower border

Roofed-in sitting area

Raised bed

Lawn

House

Porch

Street

I made the border narrow—only 1.5 metres wide—and 6.5 metres long. It got wider as time and resources allowed. Once there were plants to admire—several dahlias, a large drift of annual zinnias, some perennials such as lamb's ears (*Stachys byzantina*), cranesbill (*Geranium* spp.) and the original peonies—I felt a path was needed in front of the bed to get close to them. However, the backyard already had a path leading from the side of the house to the back of the property; it was running in the right direction, but 10 metres away from where I wanted it. In the end, my design allowed for two parallel paths: the original one and another that runs from the back door, alongside the new flower bed.

I felt it was particularly important to break up and soften the rectangular shape of the yard. One of my plans before I even moved in was to create three different areas. On an enlarged photocopy of my lot survey, I divided the backyard into three rectangles. By fall, the rectangle closest to the house was under control, with the flower bed and the two paths breaking up the lawn.

The following year, I cleared the rest of the backyard and planted shrubs—a beautybush (*Kolkwitzia amabilis*) and a few viburnums—to separate the first and second rectangles. But I wasn't satisfied with the results. The shrubs may have divided the rectangles in my mind, but to others they just looked like shrubs plopped in the middle of the backyard. Then I saw a drawing of a trellis by the 18th-century French artist J.B. Oudry, and realized that a trellis backing the shrub border would create real "bones," clearly dividing the space while still allowing a partial view of the rest of the garden. So, I installed a 2.5-metre-tall trellis across the width of the garden with two openings, one for each of the paths.

The following year, I tackled the 10-metre by 21-metre front garden. When I first moved in, it consisted of a concrete path that went straight from the sidewalk

through a lawn to the front porch. "Lawn" is an overstatement: it's more accurate to describe it as a few tufts of grass, which struggled in the shadow of a Norway maple. I removed the concrete and replaced it with a much larger, curved gravel path. I installed an island bed of hostas (tough-as-nails *H. lancifolia*), near the midpoint of the path and shade beds on either side. I needed a fence between the beds and the sidewalk, if only to stop the paper boy from taking his usual shortcut through the newly dug bed. Trelliswork such as I had built in the backyard was far too high, so I built a trellis that started low (1 metre high) along the front of the house and rose in four steps along the side garden to reach the 2.5-metre height of the trelliswork in the back.

Then I moved on to the second rectangle in the backyard. After a few failed experiments—old-fashioned roses, then a new path surrounded by large clumps of hollyhocks—the middle section remained

herbal**connections**

Let's face it: herbs, apart from perhaps parsley, basil and chives, are not used extensively. People who have herb gardens are often romantics, growing herbs in large part because of the interesting associations the plants have acquired over the centuries. They don't generally use wormwood, for example, to get rid of worms and fleas, but its fragrance may remind them that it's botanically named after Artemisia, a Greek goddess of the forest, that it's mentioned in the Bible, that it is the basic ingredient of absinthe (the favourite drink of Impressionist painters), or that it keeps venomous snakes at bay. Likewise, few modern herb gardeners believe the smell of rue wards off disease, but by inhaling the pungent scent, as herbalists Culpeper or Gerard used to do, they somehow feel closer to gardeners of the past.

a kind of grassy no-man's land for a few years.

The second year, I also installed a vegetable garden in the third rectangle. It's rather formal, with raised beds and paths covered in wood chips. I grow tomatoes, salad greens and beans; the bed is also used as a nursery for perennials grown from seed.

Five years after I moved in, I came to a decision on the middle garden: it should have either an herb garden or a pond. Both ideas were equally attractive, so I built a low trellis to divide the rectangle into two squares. In one I made a traditional four-square herb garden and in the other I installed a natural-looking pond.

At one end of the herb garden is a large pear tree, which creates too much shade for thyme or basil, but it holds lots of chives, parsley and coriander. I also

The front yard, above, once had a straight concrete sidewalk and a few struggling tufts of grass. Now it's a shady bower of daylilies, lily-of-the-valley, evening primroses and tulips. Right: inside the four-square central herb garden, white feverfew grows with sage, tarragon, chervil and potted plants. Opposite: the trellis separating the first section of the garden supports a 'John Cabot' rose.

The herb garden, below, is also home to ornamental blooms, such as the 'Fairfield Blaze' rose twining up an obelisk with white *Clematis recta*. Opposite, top: the pond's striking *Darmera palmata* produces large leaves after its blooms fade, and it combines well in spring with old-fashioned bleeding heart. Below: the herb garden clearly reveals its four-square pattern in early spring.

containersolutions

Pots are useful in any garden because they're easy to move into and out of the sun and to group together in changing arrangements. But they're especially good for making use of a surplus of plants as a result of spring division. Extra ferns that have overrun one spot can be easily uprooted and potted to grace a bare, shady corner.

Plants in pots fill empty spaces in the garden when a plant dies, or temporarily beautify a planting that hasn't worked out. Set the pot on the ground or embed it slightly to fill the gap. Lilies—one of the few perennials that do just about as well in a pot as in the ground—soon blend completely in a perennial bed.

Pots are also the easiest solution for stretching your season. Tender plants like gunnera (the monster plant frequently grown in British Columbia's Lower Mainland) or the flowering brugmansia can be grown in large pots and cut back to be brought into the cellar in winter.

Pots can change the mood of any garden. Align them and you create formality. Crowd them together and you create a feeling of informal profusion. Pots always make a garden look more established.

have a clump of French tarragon and I seed chervil in the early spring. Besides these culinary plants, yellow foxglove (*Digitalis grandiflora*), a large clump of costmary (*Tanacetum balsamita*), some comfrey, several plants of rue (*Ruta graveolens*) and a southernwood (*Artemisia abrotanum*) inhabit the herb garden. In the sunniest spots, flanking the gate to the pond, are two large rosemary plants in planters, which spend the winter in the basement under a couple of fluorescent lights.

The pond, surrounded by large stones and a bog garden, quickly became a hub for wildlife, mostly birds and dragonflies. For many years, my pride was a large clump of pitcher plant (*Sarracenia purpurea*). Unfortunately, the raccoons rule the garden by night and one spring they decided to weed out the pitcher plant.

Within six years of moving in, the garden was pretty much established. A major change took place in the seventh year, when I covered all the grass paths, except those in the vegetable garden, in gravel. In addition to uniting the various parts of the garden, as the trellis does, gravel has the effect of making the garden look more formal. That same year, I emphasized the effect by making the only remaining lawn, the strips between the two paths in the first rectangle, into a square.

The rectangular paths and the grid of the trellis create a strong, formal setting, which is softened by the plantings, profuse and informal, that climb over the trelliswork and spill over the paths.

Like most gardens designed by amateurs, mine took many years to evolve, and I've learned to adapt to changing circumstances. For example, my garden was very shady until the large willow tree next door was struck down in a storm. This required repair of the damaged fence, but also produced some sunny years. Now, as other trees mature, shade is quickly creeping back. I expect the garden will return to its original shady self in a couple of years. You have to experiment all the time to see what works. ▪

borrowedbeauty

FLOWERS ABOUND IN EVERY SEASON IN A CLASSICAL CITY GARDEN
BY JUDITH ADAM

Classic structures, such as the side-door entrance porch opposite, act as frames for the Dyers' exuberant plantings and add elegance to the overall design. The leg of land visible behind the curved metal arbour actually belongs to neighbours, but Susan and Geoffrey maintain it as garden. Left: *Arisaema candissimum*, a fragrant Jack-in-the-pulpit

The large Victorian rooming house Geoffrey and Susan Dyer bought in Toronto in the early 1980s for their family had only a postage stamp–sized garden behind it, barely 9 metres deep and 12 metres wide, a dismal prospect for the deep perennial borders they wanted. But city living is based on compromise, so, with scaled-down dreams and diminished plant lists, they set to work in the small space. Susan was prepared to sacrifice everything but lilies; Geoffrey's bottom line was a redbud tree (*Cercis canadensis*).

It soon became apparent that their skills and desires far exceeded the limits of the small space. Providence intervened in the form of neighbours Leo and Annette Zakuta, whose property extends in an L-shape behind the Dyers' lot. They were relieved to see the shabby house being restored to its former elegance, and opened up the extending leg of their backyard to the Dyers. Geoffrey and Susan expanded their planting scheme to include the Zakutas' property, blending the two spaces in a serendipitous partnership that doubled their garden area. Leo and Annette own the land, Geoffrey and Susan plant it, and both couples enjoy the view of perennial-rich borders and arbours dripping with clematis. "I know this kind of sharing can happen in country gardens," Susan says, "but it's not usual for city living."

The low hedge circling the pond was planted a few years after the pond was installed because the Dyers felt it looked bare. Clipped hedges, the clean-cut stone path and trellis fencing are typical of formal European design. Growing beside the antique edging tool below is *Lysimachia nummularia* 'Aurea'.

Garden areas near the house are formal in design and execution. A raised wood porch and two ground-level stone patios provide outdoor seating, and a formal, circular pond surrounded by clipped boxwood brings water into the garden. The formal atmosphere becomes more relaxed as one follows the stone path through archways festooned with sweet peas and clematis. Perennials billow forward and fragrant lilies spike upward in the borders, and the presence of roses is a consistent theme on all sides.

Even though Geoffrey and Susan understand the garden is a work in progress and never want it to be finished, they keep to a central design vision in their season-to-season plans. Visits to gardens in Europe convinced them that a thousand years of garden history couldn't be ignored. They were particularly impressed with the expansive perennial and rose beds of Vita Sackville-West at Sissinghurst, and the heavily planted cottage garden made by Rosemary Verey at Barnsley House, both in England. The Dyers' challenge has been to adapt this traditional garden design to their Zone 6 garden.

The classical influence is evident in the bones of their landscape. Hand-forged metal archways, dark yew hedges and square-cut stone paths organize and divide the space. The Dyers have done much of the physical labour themselves; Geoffrey can say he personally hefted each pathway stone. The strong lines delineate the deep planting beds and act as a foil to Susan's exuberant, overplanted collection of perennials, roses, daphnes, honeysuckles and flowering vines.

The distribution of creative responsibilities has a traditional resonance— Susan is in charge of anything with petals; Geoffrey concerns himself with garden structure and the maintenance of woody plants. Despite their avowed admiration for each other's skill, there is occasional trespassing. Susan will say her husband's pruning might be a bit severe. Geoffrey suggests a state of chaos reigns among the poppies. But such disagreements are minor. They're in total accord about their top priority: the health of the garden, which is paramount, even above the lust for flowers. "We just don't keep anything if it doesn't prosper here," Susan says. The Dyers, along with their

two grown daughters, spend a lot of time in the garden. "Even the cats and our dog are vulnerable to pesticides, so we don't take any chances." Varieties of phlox and bee balm consistently covered with mildew are removed. Cherished roses, like the moyesii hybrid 'Nevada', that suffer chronically from blackspot are cut back hard after flowering.

Every summer the proliferation of caterpillars feasting on the buds of antique roses, which bloom once, in June, presents a serious dilemma. Hand-picking the little green worms is a loathsome solution, although kitchen gloves considerably dull the squish impact. Insect populations in the garden seem to rise and fall in cycles, and every few years worm numbers reach plague proportions. "First you worry the caterpillars will eat all the rosebuds, and then you

worry about what spraying might do to the beneficial insects," Susan says. "And then you worry about the birds eating the poisoned insects. And by then I'm exhausted and just leave it all alone."

Soil health is a constant preoccupation. Like urban farmers, the Dyers spend as much time examining their earth as they devote to grooming the plants. Ever mindful of soil improvement, Geoffrey made the winning bid at a charity auction three years ago for three cubic metres of barely aged manure, requiring two years storage before it could be used. They are fortunate to have an ancient underground stream that delivers moisture and nutrients to secret places and has promoted monster ferns. The compost operation is a large pile of kitchen and plant trimmings kept in a far corner of the garden, turned periodically and harvested in autumn. Much to their despair, the carefully tended pile leaches rich nutrients to their nemesis, a towering Manitoba maple on a neighbour's property. The tree has begun to shade nearby perennials, and Susan predicts a less floriferous and more green-textured garden.

The garden is planted to bloom from

The garden may have a formal structure but it's never stiff or rigid; billowing plantings see to that. Susan tries new varieties every spring, and gives away extras in the fall. The terrace behind the house, where Geoffrey and Susan enjoy breakfast, holds a marble-slab table and formal iron chairs. On the step: an urn spills over with a sweet potato vine, gold coleus and trailing petunia.

late winter, when legions of small snow crocuses, anemones and primulas push through the soil, to late summer. Susan is a "bunch" planter, packing several dozen crocuses into each hole for maximum impact, and grouping primulas in tight clusters. "Canadians are so starved for colour at the end of winter, we need that over-the-top explosion of blooms, you know, like a rocket," she says. Scent is important in their garden, too; the early bulbs are accompanied by the deeply perfumed winter honeysuckle (*Lonicera fragrantissima*), February daphne (*D. mezereum*) and Korean spice viburnum (*V. carlesii*).

The garden is intensively planted in layers to create an element of surprise, inviting the viewer to venture in and find something amazing at the back of the border. Susan keeps records of what goes in and comes out of the beds, but admits the paperwork lags behind the activity of a busy season. "This is like a sampler garden. There are just so many plants here. The garden is always changing, and now becoming shadier. I find I need to adjust what I like to what I can grow."

Each spring Susan expands the collection of perennials, and then goes through an editing process in autumn, inviting friends to carry home bags stuffed with peonies, iris and other plants in need of new homes. Even though she may have loved them, it's time to try something new. While not exactly a revolving-door policy, this annual giveaway of plants helps free up space for new acquisitions. She often moves plants several times to new and better locations, and selectively eliminates those that haven't produced expected results—have failed to live up to catalogue descriptions, for example. Colour is an important quality; a colourful specimen is likely to be given another chance.

Among the few plants in the garden when they moved in was a vibrant blue-violet rose-of-Sharon shrub called 'Bluebird' (*Hibiscus syriacus* 'Bluebird') that bloomed in part-sun. Its colour and long period of bloom made it a favourite, and eventually the shrub was moved to a sunnier position, which has unleashed a landslide of fertility and self-sown seedlings. "These have been passed around to so many friends, it would be easier to give away zucchinis in August," Susan says.

Drawing on tradition, the goodwill of their neighbours and their willingness to experiment, Geoffrey and Susan have turned a small, lifeless urban plot into an oasis of colour and vitality. Each year in her quest for variety, Susan pushes the hardiness barrier a little further. "I want to grow everything, even the half-hardy plants I know won't survive here, but I try anyway," she says. One summer she planted a large container with sun-loving sedums and left it out all winter. The following spring they were all healthy and green, a climate-testing triumph.

three-season colour

Susan and Geoffrey Dyer choose plants that bloom throughout the season—one group finishes flowering as another is coming into bloom. Although Susan likes to accent her beds and borders with annuals, roses and bulbs, herbaceous perennials are the backbone of her plan. Here's what flowers in her Zone 6 garden from early spring to autumn.

EARLY SPRING
Snowdrop anemone (*A. sylvestris*)
Early columbine (*Aquilegia alpina*)
Bleeding heart (*Dicentra spectabilis*)
Shooting star (*Dodecatheon meadia*)
Barrenwort (*Epimedium* x *rubrum*)
Lenten rose (*Helleborus orientalis*)
Drumstick primrose (*Primula denticulata*)
Pasqueflower (*Pulsatilla vulgaris*)
Double bloodroot (*Sanguinaria canadensis* 'Multiplex')
Horned violet (*Viola cornuta*)

LATE SPRING
Lady's-mantle (*Alchemilla mollis*)
'Nora Barlow' columbine (*Aquilegia vulgaris* 'Nora Barlow')
Foxgloves (*Digitalis purpurea* and *D. lutea*)
Leopard's bane (*Doronicum* spp.)
Dame's rocket (*Hesperis matronalis*)
Siberian iris (*I. sibirica*)
Spring vetchling (*Lathyrus vernus*)
Virginia bluebells (*Mertensia virginica*)
Lungwort (*Pulmonaria* spp.)
Foamflower (*Tiarella wherryi* 'Oakleaf')

SUMMER
Butterfly weed (*Asclepias tuberosa*)
Clematis (*C. integrifolia*)
Tickseed (*Coreopsis verticillata* 'Golden Shower' and 'Moonbeam')
Blue corydalis (*C. flexuosa* 'Blue Panda')
Sea kale (*Crambe cordifolia*)
Delphinium (*D. grandiflorum* 'Blue Elf')
Gasplant (*Dictamnus albus*)
Purple and white coneflowers (*Echinacea purpurea* cultivars)
Foxtail lily (*Eremurus robustus*)
Alpine sea holly (*Eryngium alpinum*)
Joe-Pye weed (*Eupatorium purpureum*)
Meadowsweet (*Filipendula rubra* 'Venusta')
Cranesbill (*Geranium sanguineum* 'Max Frei')
St. John's wort (*Hypericum* spp.)
Red-hot poker (*Kniphofia* 'Primrose Beauty')
Mallow (*Lavatera* 'Barnsley')
Rose campion (*Lychnis coronaria*)
Catmint (*Nepeta* 'Blue Beauty')
Oriental poppy (*Papaver orientale* 'Perry's White')
Beard-tongue (*Penstemon* 'Garnet')
Phlox (*P. paniculata* 'Franz Schubert')
Coneflower (*Rudbeckia* 'Herbstsonne')
Perennial sage (*Salvia verticillata* 'Purple Rain')
Pincushion flower (*Scabiosa caucasica*)

LATE SUMMER TO AUTUMN
Monkshood (*Aconitum* 'Newry Blue')
Japanese anemone (*A.* x *hybrida* 'Honorine Jobert')
Italian arum (*A. italicum*)
Bugbane (*Cimicifuga simplex* 'White Pearl')
Cyclamen (*C. hederifolium* 'Bowles Apollo')
Sneezeweed (*Helenium* 'Bruno')
Sunflower (*Helianthus* x *multiflorus* 'Loddon Gold')
Yellow wax-bells (*Kirengeshoma palmata*)
Toad lily (*Tricyrtis hirta*)
Culver's root (*Veronicastrum virginicum album*)

peaceinthecity

THE HARSH SOUNDS OF THE CITY SUBSIDE IN AN ELEGANT URBAN HAVEN
BY PAMELA YOUNG

A fence with a faux-stone insert, which holds an antique fountain and basin, encloses the private garden. The climbing hydrangea growing around a fragment of old wrought-iron railing, a focal point, was inherited, but new plants were chosen for low maintenance and dependable bloom. 'Seafoam' rose, left, blooms nearly all summer.

Toronto may be Canada's largest city, but some of its best aspects, appreciated by visitors and residents alike, are the wonderful residential districts tucked away in the downtown core. Just around the corner from a busy traffic artery, you're quite likely to find yourself on a tree-lined street of beautifully maintained red-brick Victorian homes.

Ruth Bothern and Andrew Smith live on just such a street. The backyard of their century-old, semi-detached home is a gardener's *pied-à-terre*. Ruth and Andrew do their serious gardening on the weekends at their 1850s farmhouse, an hour's drive from the city, so they wanted their city garden to be a low-maintenance oasis, a quiet, leafy retreat after a hectic day. The garden is a tiny, fairly shady space, measuring not much more than 6 metres by 8 metres. Because of a six-storey condominium standing just east of the property, privacy was also an issue.

When Ruth and Andrew moved there in the mid-'90s, they weren't thrilled with the yard. Because the land slopes down and away from the house at the back, the kitchen sits a metre or so above ground level, with an exposed basement wall underneath. Previous owners had dealt with the change in grade and the unsightly wall by building a large walkout deck, which unfortunately ate up half the yard. "Being on it felt like being onstage," Andrew says. Ruth had another

Garden designer Penny Arthurs works on the principle that a few boldly scaled elements, such as the limestone slabs in the view below, make small spaces seem larger. She also created the feeling of an old site with crumbling walls by using broken pieces of rock around the raised planting. Opposite: a parrot tulip and a pink lily-flowered variety in the spring

objection: "When you sat out there your eye was drawn over the fence to the garages and condominiums beyond. You didn't feel like you had any privacy."

The couple contacted landscape designer Penny Arthurs, of the Toronto firm The Chelsea Gardener, and asked her to design a garden that would offer more privacy and resolve the grade change more effectively. Arthurs' solution was to remove the deck, increase the height of the fence around the yard and create a tiered garden that stepped down toward the back fence. Planting two fairly large trees also helped create a more secluded space. The deck, as it turned out, was covering up a bit of an eyesore. "The exposed basement wall is unfinished—it's just rubble," says Arthurs, "so I couldn't take the garden right to the base of the house." Instead, she proposed a raised planting against the back wall of the house, just beneath the glass doors of the kitchen. The owners readily agreed. They didn't mind losing that doorway to the garden because a door off to one side leading down to ground level also offered easy access. Raised plantings appealed to them for another reason: the soil of the

yard itself was clogged with old tree roots, which made it difficult to introduce plants at grade level with deep root systems of their own.

Arthurs suggested a tiered descent to ground level, to make the grade change seem less dramatic. The highest—and sunniest—part of the garden is the raised planting, containing a spectacular cascade of white 'Seafoam' roses that bloom all summer. The outer wall of this planting forms the backrest of a stone bench, which in turn leads down to a paved terrace. From the terrace, there's a final step

down to the grade level of the garden.

Arthurs needed to create a solid wall to contain the raised planting, but she knew this would pose an aesthetic problem. How could she make this wall belong in the garden without having to make the whole garden into walls? Her solution was to create the illusion of other stone structures that had tumbled into ruin. "The wall retaining the raised planting is solid," she says, "but as it goes down into the garden it's reduced to a crumbling wall—only broken pieces. I wanted to create the feeling of a forgotten site, a place

that in former times might have been occupied by a building or an old garden."

It was an idea that harmonized with the instincts of Ruth and Andrew, who like to use well-weathered manmade objects as focal points in their garden. "I love outdoor knick-knacks with patina," says Ruth. A fragment of antique wrought-iron railing encloses one corner of the paved terrace, and a filigree of 19th-century grillwork hangs on the fence as an outdoor work of art.

To give the garden the appearance of

extra size and depth, Arthurs used a couple of effective space-expanding design strategies. To draw the eye to the garden's farthest reaches, she lined up the water feature on the faux-stone back fence with the kitchen's glass doors (the ones now blocked by the raised bed). She also used extremely large limestone paving slabs from Wiarton, Ontario, in the firm belief that a carefully chosen selection of boldly scaled elements actually makes a small space seem larger.

When Ruth and Andrew bought the property, they inherited a well-established mulberry tree on the lot line in the back corner. Pruning its low-hanging branches gave them more gardening and living

space. Except for a hydrangea shrub, which now borders the terrace, and some clematis that were already climbing one wall of the house, all the plantings were new.

"We wanted lots of foliage we could see from the kitchen, and we wanted something fairly low maintenance," says Andrew. His wife, he claims, is the true gardener; his own role is more humble: "I move things around." Ruth, however, insists that her husband is, at the very least, the horticultural equivalent of a sous-chef. "He tidies, fertilizes and waters things when I get tired," she says.

They agree that the installation of a sprinkler system has made life easier for both of them—that, and the fact that few of the plants chosen require deadheading. Ruth loves bulbs, but has had problems with them. The first couple of years the tulips and daffodils put on a fine show, but the squirrels feasted on the more exotic offerings. "They ate the fritillaria," she says ruefully. The following year, only a small number of her two hundred bulbs came up. She suspects that lack of sun and overwatering were to blame. On a

watermagic

Water features are especially appropriate in urban settings, where the peaceful sound of trickling water, though subtle, does a wonderful job of masking traffic noise.

In the midtown garden of Ruth Bothern and Andrew Smith, a terra-cotta lavabo pleases the ear as well as the eye. Its prominent position—centred on the back fence, on an axis with the kitchen's bay window (see photo on facing page)—makes it a graceful focal point year-round. The basin was created by slicing a mid-19th-century antique urn down the middle and backing one of the halves with metal. The water-spouting cherub mounted above it dates from the same era.

Landscape designer Penny Arthurs wanted something visually solid on which to mount the lavabo, the garden's main ornamental element. Putting up a solid wall wasn't possible because of the public laneway behind the property, so Arthurs commissioned a local artist to create a trompe l'oeil stone wall using acrylic paint on a type of board normally used for outdoor billboards. An ultraviolet protectant coats the finished artwork to keep it from fading. "This is one stone wall that will never need repointing," says Ruth.

The gentle sounds of water falling into the lavabo, made by cutting an antique urn in half, screen the sound of nearby city traffic.

happier note, the Boston ivy and two types of clematis—'Nelly Moser' and 'Frances Rivis'—did spectacularly well.

The garden is charming in all seasons. Soon after the pale purple, miniature lilacs bordering the terrace come out in early June, the 'Seafoam' roses start blooming like mad. "This rose would take over the whole garden if it had a chance," Arthurs says. In high summer, the pale blooms of astilbe and Oriental lilies stand out against the dark green foliage.

Although Ruth is partial to annuals, on Arthurs' advice she resisted the urge to go overboard with them. In fact, the only type she usually plants in her city garden was the deep blue 'Victoria' salvia (*Salvia farinacea* 'Victoria'). When annuals are used to fill in the spaces that are a fact of life in any new garden, Arthurs notes, perennials won't spread as well.

She selected a serviceberry (*Amelanchier canadensis*) and a honeylocust (*Gleditsia* spp.) as new trees for the garden. In addition to producing a snowy mantle of blossoms in early spring, the serviceberry has leaves that turn to tones of rust and red in autumn—a striking contrast to the locust's, which are yellow in fall.

On a warm summer evening, this leafy, rose-scented garden is a delightfully serene place. After nightfall, the perfectly positioned outdoor lighting reveals the outlines of the stone "ruins" and accentuates the sculptural relief of the water feature on the back fence. The soft splash of water trickling into the ornamental basin screens out the sounds of traffic, and the big, bustling city beyond the fence all but disappears. ∎

goodgarden bones

Well-designed gardens have a good basic structure. Because of its good bones, this one looks as inviting in winter as in summer. Properly placed shrubs and urns and a handsome bench provide focal points, and a lovely door breaks the sterile side passage.

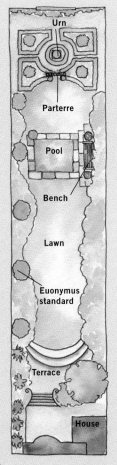

Garage

Urn

Parterre

Pool

Bench

Lawn

Euonymus standard

Terrace

House

Because of its good basic design, this classic garden retains its sculptural beauty even during the dreariest winter. Toronto landscape designer Brenda Dinnick and her husband bought their 1889 Georgian-style house more than a decade ago, and during year-long renovations Brenda had time to assess the garden. It had been sadly neglected, but it contained a stellar collection of mature perennials and shrubs, carefully selected for

succession of bloom. Brenda added hardscaping: a patio, gravel pathway and stone wall. She repaired the pool, pulled down a fence, erected a handsome iron arbour and transformed the rickety garage into a trellised focal point. As a transition from the house, a wide, welcoming terrace with a graceful sweep of steps was created, echoed at the opposite end by a formal boxwood parterre with a semicircular curve.

The side beds were sculpted into a serpentine shape to create the illusion of greater width, and existing vines and shrubs were pruned to give them a more

A formal house like this one benefits from symmetry in the garden design. Divide a long garden into sections, don't overplant, and keep shrubs carefully pruned to maintain interesting shapes. It's important to pay attention to detail in a classic garden.

architectural shape. Brenda played up the narrow, mysterious side passageway to the garden from the street by installing a tall, black door with an antique knocker. When visitors walk through it, they're momentarily hemmed in by a dark green wall of pyramidal cedars, and then the beckoning garden unfolds.

Here are Brenda Dinnick's guidelines for achieving good basic design.
• Start with structure. Define the space with fences, hedges, walls, planters and beds. Add plants and flowers when the design is defined.
• Keep the architecture of the house in mind when planning the design: emphasize structure and symmetry for a Georgian house; use loose, billowy plantings for a cottage; think in terms of a minimal garden for a modern house.

• Work with your surroundings. For example, huge rocks and mini-meadows tend to look odd in urban settings.
• A graceful transition from house to garden is important. Set the terrace fairly low to gain privacy.
• A change of level adds appeal to a garden; even a step or two can make a difference.
• Gardens, like stories, should have a beginning, a middle and an end. If both ends tie together visually—perhaps with echoing curves or repeating elements—the space will feel harmonious. ▪

classic reflections

A mirror fools the eye into thinking a garden is twice as big, especially if it's placed within a false arbour, as is the mirror here. It acts as both a focal point in the garden and downplays the imposing house next door by reflecting the owner's own home.

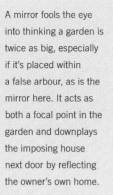

Mirrors in a garden draw attention to its attractive aspects, such as a prized plant, a piece of statuary or a pool. They can also make a small garden appear larger, or draw light into a dark space. Here are some design ideas from experts.

• A mirror is particularly effective if it's integrated into a setting among trees, which act as a ceiling for the space. Even a large mirror is less immediately visible framed this way.

• Mirrors set into a trelliswork fence give a narrow garden the illusion of width. Set a few shrubs and perennials in front to suggest another garden "room" beyond.

• Place the mirror so it reflects greenery, rather than the back door of your house, and angle it so you don't see your own reflection as you approach it directly.

• A strip of mirror is a great way to increase the impact of a water feature. Place it low, embedded in the plantings around a small pool, or install it on a fence behind a fountain to double the impact of the play of water.

• Mirrors cladding the base of planter boxes in a roof garden make them look like they're floating. ▪

mirror basics

The mirror opposite is an antique door frame backed with plywood and sealed with clear silicone. It gives an Alice-in-Wonderland effect, implying another world beyond, and is still in good shape after a decade in place.

Using mirrors in the garden is a rather new idea, so you won't find preframed mirrors in garden centres. Here are some tips for setting them up.

• You can use heavy architectural mirror glass, but it's expensive and harder to find than standard mirror. Use the best quality available, thicker than you'd need indoors (4-mm rather than 3-mm thick).

• A less expensive option is mirror made from acrylic, which is lighter, bendable (an advantage if you want the mirror to curve) and available in tints such as gold, bronze and copper. But the material doesn't last as long as glass.

• Have the mirror cut to the size you want and attach it to a panel of plywood with clips or an adhesive suitable for use with glass.

• Seal the edges with silicone labelled for outdoor use. This protects the cut edges of the glass from moisture and provides a cushion between the mirror's edges and the frame.

• Attach the mirror to a structure—such as a frame made to resemble an arbour—that can handle the weight and won't be affected by wind.

- Don't allow the bottom edge to rest on the soil or paving stones that might shift with frost.

- To prevent birds from flying into the mirror, place it among shrubs that branch over its surface, or behind a solid-looking garden ornament. ▪

container magic

Windowbox planter

You don't need to be rich or possessed with magic powers to own unusual plant containers. Just treat garden-variety pots, like the simple oval plastic planter at top right, or the clay herb pot, to some paint. More ornate planters can disguise themselves as classic cast iron.

Stone urns, cast-iron planters and bronze or metal containers are part of the design in classic gardens. Painted, aged terra-cotta has an appeal of its own. But many of these accessories are hard to find and downright expensive. Here are some ways to transform ordinary old or new containers into costly looking classical designs.

For the painted finishes, first clean and prime pots using the basic instructions that follow.

Then use any of the easy finishing techniques. The metal finishes need only cleaning with TSP (trisodium phosphate), without the paint primer.

The Basics: Thoroughly scrub new or old containers inside and out using TSP (available at paint and hardware stores) or warm, soapy water. Rinse and let dry.

Containers with shiny, smooth surfaces, such as plastic or resin, must be roughed up with fine-to-medium sandpaper. Remove rust or peeling paint from metal surfaces with fine steel wool. Apply all-purpose exterior latex primer (such as Benjamin Moore's Fresh Start).

ra-cotta herb pot

Resin or plaster planter

stylish solutions

Note: If the container is made of non-galvanized metal, use non-water-based primer or red oxide, and then follow with rust-proofing paint.

For the final finish, use exterior latex or acrylic latex paint in low- to soft-sheen paint finishes (such as Benjamin Moore's Moor-Gard, Latex House Paint and Acrylic Latex House and Trim Paint, which is also suitable for primed metal surfaces).

TERRA-COTTA HERB POT

(previous page) For a weathered look, dip a brush into the paint colour desired, remove excess from the brush on a paper towel, and apply randomly over the pot, building paint as desired. Leave some areas of terra-cotta exposed. Stencil or write the names of herbs on the pot.

WINDOWBOX PLANTER

(previous page) An ordinary resin planter can be transformed into a rustic "stone" trough with Natural Stone FX, a ready-mixed, water-based plaster product. Using a brush, apply the product randomly to cover the entire surface. In separate containers, dilute small amounts of green and yellow paint using one part water to two parts paint; apply each colour sparingly with a brush or rag until you achieve the desired mossy, aged look. Immediately remove excess paint with a clean rag.

RESIN/PLASTER ROCOCO PLANTER

(previous page) A purchased faux-stone planter takes on the look of classic cast iron with just a little black paint. Apply two coats of paint and rub some off the high spots for an aged look.

For a worn or antique effect, use a slapdash approach when applying faux finishes. Even coats of colour will look unnatural, and the under colours won't show through as well. Apply thin coats—it's easier to add colour than remove it later.

METAL FINISHES

If you like the look of antique metal but want a container that's more practical, it's easy to create convincing lookalikes. All it takes is a coat or two of paint—you don't have to be an artist. In fact, a slapdash approach is best—if you're too careful when applying the finish, it looks fake. Finishes are quick to apply and the inexpensive materials are easily readily available in paint and craft stores.

ANTIQUE PEWTER FINISH

Apply a mottled blue-green coat to a terra-cotta pot (as in antique bronze instructions at right). Let dry overnight.

Take a rag or piece of paper towel, twist it over your forefinger and dip it into a pot of silver gilt paste. Rub the paste on the container (photo c), working it in one area at a time, aiming for a mottled effect; apply in thin layers, pausing frequently to assess your work, until you've achieved the desired effect. Small patches of terra-cotta and verdigris should be visible.

Allow to dry overnight, and then rub lightly with a clean cloth or paper towel to burnish the finish. Apply several coats of varnish, following the manufacturer's directions.

ANTIQUE BRONZE FINISH

Squeeze a bit of blue-green paint into a plastic tub. Dab the tip of a clean foam brush in the paint to pick up a small amount. Remove excess paint by dabbing the brush on a folded paper towel.

Apply a mottled coat of the blue-green paint to a terra-cotta pot—aim for a haphazard effect that mimics the look of verdigris (photo a). Dab paint randomly in blotches over the pot until about three-quarters of the surface is covered. Paint the inside to a depth of at least 5 centimetres, but not the bottom of the pot. Allow paint to dry overnight.

Squeeze a small amount of bronze, copper or gold paint into a plastic tub. Apply it as you did the blue-green paint: in patches and sparingly (photo b). Make sure some of the blue-green colour shows through, as well as bits of the original terra-cotta.

When you're satisfied with the effect, allow the pot to dry overnight. To weatherproof, apply several coats of polyurethane varnish, following the manufacturer's directions.

RUSTED IRON FINISH

The materials used for this effect are corrosive: wear protective gloves and eyewear at all times; cover your work surface well with newspaper; and work in a well-ventilated area.

Squeeze a small amount of Instant Iron (powdered iron in a liquid suspension) into a plastic tub. Using a foam craft brush, apply an even coat to a terra-cotta container. Allow half an hour to dry and then apply a second coat, taking care to cover any areas of terra-cotta that show through. Paint the inside of the container to a depth of 5 centimetres. Allow the base coat to cure overnight.

Pour a small amount of Liquid Rust (a corrosive liquid that oxidizes the iron) into a plastic tub. Dip a foam brush into the liquid and then brush liberally over the terra-cotta container. For a natural effect, brush the liquid on unevenly, concentrating on areas where rust might occur naturally, such as the rim. Wait several hours for the rust to develop. In the meantime, cover the plastic tub and wrap the foam brush in plastic wrap so the Liquid Rust doesn't dry out.

If the rust effect isn't pronounced enough in some areas, paint on more Liquid Rust (photo d) and allow it to develop as above.

Allow the pot to dry overnight. Apply several coats of varnish, following the manufacturer's directions. ■

B   C   D

Bold and beautiful gardens made by plant lovers abound in urban areas

perennial gardens

108 BREAKING THE RULES

114 THE EDUCATION OF
     A GARDENER

120 A FRESH START

PLANT SOLUTIONS
126 PLANTS FOR FOUR
     SEASONS
128 THE ROOT OF GOOD
     GARDENING

STYLISH SOLUTIONS
130 YEAR-ROUND GARDEN

breaking
therules

A KELOWNA COUPLE GROWS A JUNGLE IN THE ARID OKANAGAN
BY SUZANNE ANDERTON

Gerry Herron likes exotic plants in tropical settings, and his man-made Zone 5 jungle supports an incredible number of tender varieties. His secret? A winter garden room, a couple of strong sons and a dolly for moving heavy pots. Three ponds with a tropical look also grace the dramatic garden vistas. Left: *Datura meteloides*

Gerry and FranCeen Herron's garden isn't suited to the kind of climate the Okanagan Valley provides: it doesn't have the right soil conditions, it gets only 30 centimetres of rain a year, and there are too many plants crammed into the spaces allotted to them.

Gerry's philosophy is that anything is possible, and he breaks all the conventional rules, achieving a lush, tropical enclave in his Zone 5 garden. By providing plenty of indoor accommodation in winter and paying attention to the idiosyncratic nuances of tropicals year-round, his garden thrives against all odds.

Family and friends have dubbed Gerry the "Jurassic Gardener" because of the giant-leafed tropical plants he grows. The view of the front of the house, at the end of a quiet street, gives little indication of this, however. Here, in the only area that gets much sun, wide perennial beds with a fairly traditional look do nothing to prepare you for the dramatic vistas in the back. Only the enormous gunnera (*Gunnera manicata*) beside a pond near the front door and the profusion of daturas (*Datura meteloides*) hint at what's in store. From under a white trellis on the east side of the house beside a large pond, you catch glimpses of gigantic plants both in and out of the water, and suddenly the term *Jurassic* starts to have real meaning.

You are entering a jungle—a tropical one.

The charming English-style house and entrance garden are deceiving: a closer look reveals exotic vines everywhere—wisteria, passionflower, bougainvillea and *Rhodochiton atrosanguineum*, seen at left on facing page. Variegated ginger, lower photo opposite, jade plant, hibiscus, banana palms and New Zealand flax are among the garden's summer residents.

interspersed throughout the garden—rhododendrons, azaleas, tree mallow (*Lavatera*), weigelas, rodgersia, hellebores and hydrangeas all thrive in the perennial beds. The foliage of numerous rex begonias looks spectacular against the dark green backdrop of the shady parts of the southeast-facing rear garden. *Solenostemon* 'Solar Series', quite tolerant of the sun that occasionally peeks through, has been propagated in the greenhouse, and dozens of potted specimens form a tiny hedge of brilliant colour along the pathway on the east side of the house. Vines grow everywhere—many clematis, wisteria, bougainvillea,

morning glory (*Ipomoea*), passionflower (*Passiflora*) and ivy. There's not a surface left unplanted or unadorned with some little treasure that FranCeen has found. Birdhouses, benches, garden signs, reflecting glass and a twig bicycle add to the ambience without distracting from the abundant growth.

A tour around the garden is a long one, not because there's far to go, but because there is so much that is fascinating and unfamiliar. And then again, you want to leave lots of time to listen to Gerry talk about the plants and, when FranCeen is out of earshot, the plans he has for adding more.

tropicaltips

Avoid repotting very large plants by using very large pots (with good drainage) to begin with. But proceed with care—if a tropical plant is potbound, pot up two sizes only or the plant might put all its energy into growing more roots.

Use a light soil mix—for example a 50/50 blend of mushroom manure and topsoil. If mushroom compost is not available in your area, try combining half peat moss–based soilless mix and half sterilized potting soil.

If you have an automatic watering system, save yourself hand-watering time by placing pots within its range, but check regularly to ensure that the system is doing the job.

During the summer, fertilize plants once a week—use manure tea for large-leafed plants and a 10-60-10 (or the more common 15-30-15) formula for flowering plants.

Overwatering is your plants' worst enemy. Do not allow them to become water-logged; during winter, keep plants quite dry.

Aphids can be a problem with tropicals. Remove by hand or by spraying with a hose. Keep a sharp lookout for white flies and spider mites, which can be a problem when tropicals are brought indoors. ■

theeducationof agardener

A BEGINNER LEARNS TO BLEND COLOUR, TEXTURE AND SCENT
BY LAURA LANGSTON

A graceful plum tree frames the pathway to a birdbath in one of Lily Maxwell's lovely borders, glowing in the late-day sun. Beauty in form and texture is as much a priority in her garden as are pleasing colour combinations. Right: lily-of-the-Nile

Victoria's scenic drive winds along miles of ocean past grand homes, many of them surrounded by stunning gardens. It's fitting that the garden of Lily Maxwell should be along the route, for beauty is her first priority. "My dad grew vegetables in our front yard, and it really embarrassed me," she remembers. "So now I don't grow anything practical."

Lily became interested in gardening about 16 years ago when she and her husband, Glenn, moved to the 2,000-square-metre property. Realizing the 1930s house needed a lot of costly work that would have to wait, she decided instead to spruce up the sunny, south-facing lot. The property was large, and there were many changes she wanted to make.

So she wouldn't feel overwhelmed by the task, Lily decided to develop one area each summer. "To attempt anything else would have been crazy, as well as expensive" she says. Today, mixed borders filled with perennials, ornamental grasses, bulbs, interesting shrubs and trees curve around a sloping lawn. Because of a small upward slope, the house seems to sit on a slight hill. The slope is less pronounced in the back, but the views are just as beautiful—from the deck one sees another sweep of lawn and wide, enticing borders that vary from subtle and serene to vibrant and colourful.

coolweathercolour

Perennial hellebores are superb shade or semi-shade plants with handsome palmate leaves and large, waxy blooms that make excellent cut flowers. Growing 45 to 90 centimetres tall and flowering from late January to March in British Columbia, and from March through April elsewhere, they add a touch of colour to the winter garden. Ideally, they should be grown in slightly raised beds to make it easier to view their nodding flowers. Hardiness of cultivars varies from Zones 4 to 9.

Two of the most popular hellebores are Lenten rose (*Helleborus orientalis*), which produces white, or various shades of red or pink flowers, and Christmas rose (*H. niger*), which produces white or greenish-white flowers that turn purple as they mature.

Connoisseurs appreciate the evergreen *H. argutifolius*, which reaches 90 centimetres and produces tough, glossy leaves with serrated edges and dense bunches of bright, apple-green flowers in early spring. They're also fond of *H. x 'Sternii'* (45 centimetres, Zone 7), which produces blue-grey leaves and rose-tinted flowers; another favourite is *H. foetidus* (60 centimetres), or the stinking hellebore, which smells mildly skunky—but only if you put your nose very close to the yellow-green flowers.

Pair hellebores with snowdrops and delicate spring bulbs or early-blooming rhododendrons. They require fertile, humus-rich soil that's well drained but retains some moisture in summer. Clumps may be divided in spring or fall, although hellebores hate to be disturbed and may not recover for several years. *H. niger* and *H. orientalis* are evergreen, and old, bedraggled leaves should be cut off in late winter, when buds appear, to allow for growth.

In the beginning, though, Lily wasn't sure what to do, so she hired a designer to create a rockery. After the first season, the thyme, dianthus and aubrieta the designer put in didn't thrill her, and following the dazzling spring display of rhododendrons and azaleas, the garden was colourless. Lily began to study gardening on her own, reading books and visiting other gardens. Today she designs in her head or while she's on her knees in the soil, often moving plants in full bloom. "I take up lots of soil around the roots and water like crazy afterwards," she says.

The original rockery has been widened and filled with heathers, drumstick alliums, a cutleaf maple, some evergreens, small-leafed rhododendrons and lavender. Other favourite rockery plants include *Geranium renardii*, for the nubby texture of its big leaves; *Cerinthe major*, a striking honeywort with navy-blue-tinged flower bracts; and *Deschampsia cespitosa*

Red, white and green plants form a striking combination of colours on opposite page, lower left: in the foreground, cardinal flower and lambs-ears, with white Peegee hydrangea blossoms and Japanese bloodgrass in the middle, backed by creamy grasses. Left: *Hellebores orientalis* Below: the elegant garden shed

around me," she says.

Lily believes there are two types of collectors—those who plant unusual things but don't put plants together well, and those who offer up beautiful displays but use uninteresting plants. She aims to bring the two together. That doesn't mean buying a plant just because it's collectible—plants she "absolutely loves" are the only ones given a patch of earth. Life, she says, is too short to live with mistakes.

Once the front was underway, Lily moved to the shady west side, where barren grass grew. It and a huge tower of English ivy nearby were removed. With what she calls beginner's luck, she bought two fatsias in one-gallon pots and lots of ferns. "I put them in and added some hostas, and that area has remained relatively unchanged."

Most of the rest of the garden has not. Eventually, Lily made her way around the entire back garden and up the other side, digging, designing, widening, planting and rearranging flower borders. By then, it was time to redefine the front garden.

The back garden reflects Lily's belief that a garden should vary from place to place. Close to the house, the feeling is formal and structured, with small English boxwoods, paths and planters. Against the deck, formality is softened with a pale pink 'New Dawn' rose, the fragrant, apricot 'Royal Sunset' rose and two white clematis—*recta* and 'Miss Bateman'. Dwarf white astilbes grow at ground level. Farther from the house, the garden is less formal. The west side is shady, restful, almost muted. Plants near the garden house, where tools, bikes and patio furniture are stored, emphasize foliage—hostas, including 'Frances Williams', 'August Moon', 'Fragrant Bouquet' and 'Patriot'; the Japanese perennial shrub *Kirengeshoma palmata*, with clear-yellow flowers; and a number of hydrangeas, including her favourite

'Northern Lights', a grass whose stripes are first gold and green, then gently fade to creamy white and produce shimmering, cloud-like flower heads. A few of the original rockery plants remain, including a hard-pruned honeysuckle and Japanese anemones.

Though she began with a soft palette of greys, blues, purples and whites, Lily has introduced yellow, gold and chartreuse-toned foliage plants. In the rockery, these include golden oregano and *Euphorbia amygdaloides* var. *robbiae*, which produces swells of chartreuse flowers in spring.

Plants must earn a place in Lily Maxwell's garden. They must never be invasive brutes, and they should offer year-round interest or have one outstanding feature, such as striking foliage, shape, colour or scent. One plant that performs several roles is the California tree poppy (*Romneya coulteri*). A perennial that can reach 2.1 metres in height and dies back in a hard winter, the romneya blooms from June to fall. Lily says it has

everything going for it—unusual blue-green foliage, incredible scent and stunning white and yellow, 13-centimetre blooms. "It's worth looking for the cultivar 'White Cloud' because its foliage is more striking," she says.

Another plant Lily loves for its architectural foliage is *Melianthus major*. Sometimes called the honey plant (or the peanut butter plant because of the smell of its leaves), *M. major*'s glaucous blue foliage and saw-toothed, pink-edged leaves give it a prehistoric look. Lily planted this show-stopper with a blue-green rue, an upright, silvery curry plant, *Lysimachia punctata* 'Alexander', several euphorbias and a green santolina.

She plans her beautifully designed plant combinations on instinct. "I've come to appreciate beautiful things

Plants must earn a place in Lily's garden. They must be well behaved and offer one outstanding feature if they can't provide year-round interest. The border below features *Echinops* 'Arctic Glow' and phlox 'Nora Leigh'. Below right: annual million bells and sweet potato vine fill an oval planter.

'Annabelle'. Nearby, the striped blue-and-white flowers of a willow gentian (*Gentiana asclepiadea*) echo the white of the hydrangea and the blue of an adjacent bellflower. More blue is provided by Himalayan blue poppies.

Tucked here and there are brunneras, perennials Lily loves for their hairy, heart-shaped leaves topped in spring by beautiful forget-me-not blue flowers. She also cherishes hellebores.

The pleasing combinations in Lily's back garden are endless: a well-behaved mound of lady's-mantle growing beside the perennial geranium 'Phoebe Noble' offers interesting leaf contrast, and the pink blooms of the geranium often appear at the same time as the frothy chartreuse sprays of the lady's-mantle. In another spot, her plan to pair the geranium 'Ann Folkard' with artemisia 'Powis Castle' was altered when the geranium intertwined with a golden variegated sage. It was a happy accident.

Visible from the deck, *Astrantia* 'Ruby Wedding' flourishes below a 'Double Otto' fuchsia. Hummingbirds flock to cardinal flower (*Lobelia cardinalis*), a showy, late-summer perennial with upright spikes of scarlet flowers; they also like the tropical shrub *Cestrum elegans*, with its purplish-red flowers. A chocolate cosmos (*Cosmos atrosanguineus*) has been planted in front of *Euphorbia dulcis* 'Chameleon', which produces bur-

gundy-purple foliage and greenish-yellow flower clusters flushed with purple. The two plants are accented by the maroon leaves of *Hylotelephium* 'Matrona'.

One of the reasons Lily can grow chocolate cosmos as a perennial is because she faces a huge challenge in her garden: rocks. Lots of them. They provide the drainage needed by tender perennials with tuberous roots, such as chocolate cosmos and *Melianthus major*, which can rot in frozen or wet soil, but they also make it extraordinarily difficult to establish garden beds. "In one spot out front, you couldn't get the shovel in more than half an inch," says Lily. She hired a contractor who dug for 16 hours while she put in 6 hours of her own. When the rocks were hauled away, they filled a small pickup truck.

After a few years, about the time Lily had become "a real, serious gardener," she realized some of the trees had to go. "You really should look at your trees first," she admits. Thirty trees have been removed over the past few years, including fifteen 15-metre-high Lombardy poplars. This gave Lily's neighbour the water view he craved, and allowed Lily to overhaul a bed that had never produced because of the invasive poplar roots. More than anything, however, the trees' removal allowed her to plant a ginkgo, dogwoods (*Cornus* 'Eddie's White Wonder', *C. kousa* var. *chinensis*) and *Stewartia pseudocamellia*. The witch hazels (*Hamamelis* x *intermedia*), which she adores, include 'Pallida' and 'Arnold Promise', both with fragrant, sulfur-yellow flowers, and 'Diane', which has coppery-red flowers. They bloom in late winter when most things are dormant.

Providing a glimpse of loveliness in winter is a priority for Lily. "No matter when people visit," she says, "I want them to be inspired by unusual plants and interesting combinations, but most of all to be left with the feeling of beauty." ■

afreshstart

A DEDICATED GARDENER REMAKES HER PLOT AND SHARES HER WISDOM
BY SUZANNE ZWARUN

Joan Langley has accomplished the dream of many gardeners: she's renovated her garden twice. The first version left her unhappy because it lacked bloom, so she started again. Now she shares what she learned in the process with other gardeners. Left: annual yellow daisies and 'Ville de Lyons' clematis

Lunch over, Joan Langley leads her flock of fledgling gardeners back into the garden at her home in central Edmonton. The half-dozen women attending Joan's seminar are firing questions at her as they make their way down the interlocking red brick path on the north side of the house. An area like this, sandwiched between fence and wall, is dead space in many gardens, but Joan has yellow plumes 2 metres tall blooming here. She identifies the giants as two kinds of ligularia—*L. dentata* 'Desdemona' and *L. steno-cephala* 'The Rocket'—and tells her students that yellow flowers act like rays of sunshine in a shady nook. Lady's-mantle (*Alchemilla mollis*) catches someone's eye. Joan points out how even a splash of rain scatters drops that look like diamonds on the leaves.

Joan has won many awards from the Edmonton Horticultural Society since she first entered the group's annual gardening contest in 1994, but it was volunteering her house for a house and garden tour in 1996 that gave her the idea for gardening seminars. "Five hundred people came through on the tour—and did they have questions! I stood here for four hours and talked nonstop. People are hungry for advice," she says. They need help visualizing what the plant in a 4-inch pot at a nursery will grow into. "They come away from the sessions enthused, happy, excited."

The large stream that traverses the garden was an integral part of the first renovation, but it had a harsh concrete lining that couldn't be softened with plants. In the reconstruction, Joan kept the shape but had the concrete jackhammered out and replaced with more deeply laid vinyl hidden by many sizes of stones and gravel. The stream babbles gently like a natural brook, and runs under two wooden bridges and past two waterfalls. The plants, even stately lilies, delphinium and 'The Rocket' ligularia, combine with grasses and groundcovers for a woodland effect. The Zone 3 garden never fails to draw oohs and aahs from visitors.

The seminars are held in Joan's garden, which reflects her careful eye for texture, contour and complementary colours. When people first step through the gate of the 1913 home just north of the North Saskatchewan River, they gasp at finding themselves in a woodland glade, complete with babbling brook. Towering trees—a century-old 18-metre butternut, 12-metre Scotch pines—make up the structure of the garden. But it's the stream, built in the 1980s and almost completely reconstructed in 1994, that is

truly captivating. Wending its way the east-west length of the yard, it travels under two bridges and passes two falls where the water courses over sandstone outcroppings. Waterlilies float in four tranquil ponds, and stands of ribbon grass, maidenhair fern and globeflower (*Trollius* spp.) grow on the marshy banks.

Joan has erased all trace of turf from her backyard. She urges students to try the dwarf hybrids of gladiolus because these midgets can withstand the prairie winds that beat down the taller varieties.

"They're cheap," she tells them. "Treat them like annuals." On the other hand, she advises gardeners to save by getting lilies at the Alberta Regional Lily Society's annual September sale, where members' surplus bulbs go for about $5, maybe a little more. "And lavatera seeds grow like stinkweed; don't buy plants."

Joan believes in getting the biggest bang for the buck—'Desdemona' ligularia looks great from the moment its purple-tinged leaves poke through the ground in spring, she says, and the dense seedheads of astilbe create dramatic-looking triangles against the white background of a snowy garden.

Two hours after the five-hour seminar is supposed to have ended, Joan is still fielding questions. Best to move iris before the end of August—the roots need at least six weeks to grow before the first frost, she warns one woman. "I'm fairly new to gardening," says another woman, surveying Joan's garden enviously. "I've only been at it seven years."

Joan hasn't been gardening as long as that, but she has educated herself with the intensity of the obsessed. She remedied her lack of academic horticultural background by extensive reading. "You read, you look, you learn the Latin. Eventually, it becomes as familiar as your own family tree." She has a library of more than a hundred reference books. "When you're doing something that resonates with you, it's not spent energy—it gives you energy," she says.

Growing up in a family that preserved much of its own food, she planted her own 7.5-metre by 30-metre vegetable garden as a young woman living in a rented house. Raising produce did not become a passion, however, and she abandoned gardening when she discovered how impractical it was to have huge quantities of vegetables maturing at the same time.

Joan bought her present house in 1980. The focal point of the yard was a concrete

Large rocks, seen at the stream's edges, below, help hide the pumps that recirculate the water. Joan uses many colours of bloom to add bright notes to the garden, including the dianthus bordering the stream, 'Red Ensign' dwarf morning glory at left, and the pretty blue-and-white columbine, which echoes the colours of the house, far left. Below left: 'Vera Jamieson' sedum

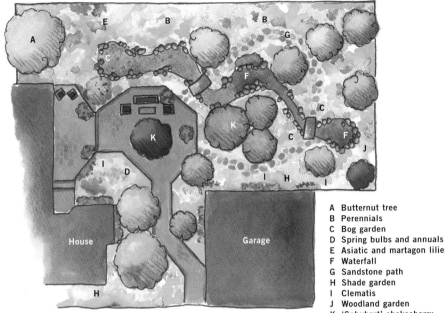

A   Butternut tree
B   Perennials
C   Bog garden
D   Spring bulbs and annuals
E   Asiatic and martagon lilies
F   Waterfall
G   Sandstone path
H   Shade garden
I   Clematis
J   Woodland garden
K   'Schubert' chokecherry
    (Prunus virginiana 'Schubert')

dog run for the German shepherd that had lived there, and the rest of the 20-metre by 39-metre property was a tangle of common lilac, quantities of quackgrass and some straggly old Manitoba maples (*Acer negundo*), also called box elders. When she started renovations on the house a few years later, Joan made a clean sweep of the yard. "It took a backhoe and a chain to drag out the lilacs," she says. Only the butternut tree (*Juglans cinerea*), a native of the eastern U.S. that resembles the black walnut, was spared. Joan imagines someone acquired a nut somehow and stuck it in the ground when the house was built. Its offspring now populate the neighbourhood.

decoratingoutdoors

"My garden is like an extension of my house," says Joan Langley, who carries the old-fashioned styles and colours she uses in her 1913 home to the outdoors.

The luxuriously large wicker armchairs on the patio have cushions that match the white house trimmed in Wedgwood blue. An antique letterbox flanks the front steps; an old-fashioned cast-iron birdbath hangs from a pine tree. The lattice top on the white fence is Wedgwood blue. Three free-standing trellises, also trimmed in blue, screen the top part of the patio, creating a secluded room.

Experts say outdoor furniture has to be functional, durable and weather-resistant. That doesn't have to mean moulded plastic, says Joan, who found cast-iron reproductions of antiques that are both serviceable and in keeping with the style of the house. Even her delicate-looking wicker-and-wood settee, chairs and coffee table are surprisingly sturdy. In a heavy rain, Joan throws a tarp over the group, and, years after they were purchased, the hand-painted motifs on the furniture are still bright. "Esthetics are the first thing, but I also look for good, solid pieces. Comfort is important. That's what I hate about plastic. It doesn't have the same feel."

Joan prefers pots, jars, urns and baskets made of ceramic, terra-cotta and wicker to statuary, partly because she feels classical figures would not suit her woodland setting. "The way stuff is used is odd sometimes," she says. "People will put a Japanese pagoda into a garden that doesn't have anything else Japanese."

At the same time, great drama can be created using a piece that contrasts with the background. Joan has a 90-centimetre-tall cobalt blue urn in one bed. Coral and salmon peonies bloom around it in the early summer; yellow rudbeckia springs up in the fall. "The urn is a focal point because it's such an intense blue," she says. "Nothing else in the garden is that colour. It really draws your eye."

Later in the '80s, after south and west wings had been added to the house, Joan knew something had to be done with the yard. A landscaper was hired who determined she had a penchant for privacy, liked the sound of water and wanted the feeling of not being in the city. He enclosed the yard with a high, lattice-topped fence, plotted the course of the stream and planted a forest of trees. "It was entirely trees, lawn and shrubs," Joan recalls. "I didn't know how to spell the word *perennial* back then."

The landscaping, including a patio of interlocking pavers, was expensive, but

Joan soon realized it was scant improvement on the dog run. "By 1990, everything was overgrown, improperly placed, lacking bloom. It was not visually appealing. No definition—shrubs intermingled in grand confusion. There were potentilla in the shade of the butternut and they never bloomed at all. And the lawn wouldn't grow under all those trees."

That's when Joan started her self-education. "I discovered there was an awful lot more than shrubs. I noticed the sameness of Edmonton gardens and decided there was something dreadfully wrong with this picture."

She blames the sameness on landscapers' reliance on a handful of fast-growing indestructibles—junipers, potentilla, spirea, mock orange and Mayday trees (*Prunus padus* var. *commutata*). "You see far too many of them," says Joan. Left to their own devices, they often look as

back-lanegardens

In the older parts of many Western cities, back lanes run behind the houses to provide access to detached garages and for garbage pickup. They also offer a bit of garden space—for a small vegetable patch, a few extra tomato or potato plants, or for an array of pretty annuals.

Laneway gardening has its hazards, though. One woman who lined her lane with iris came back an hour later to find every plant gone. Joan Langley forestalls that problem by putting in plants that are prolific self-seeders—mounds of blue flax flanked by old-fashioned pink poppies. She also recommends enthusiastic self-seeders such as calendula, shasta daisy and *Campanula carpatica*—"Little blue bells that bloom and bloom," she says.

messy as an unmade bed to a mind as tidy as Joan's. "They attract every disease and pest going. If there are tent caterpillars around, they undulate up and down a Mayday in rows."

In 1993, deciding she had made an expensive mistake, Joan started her garden again, almost from scratch. The shrubs were yanked out and donated to friends in the country. Sixteen trees remain, but Joan's least favourites are gone. The lawn was eliminated. Healthy helpings of topsoil, peat moss and mushroom manure were added and large flower beds created. In 1994, Joan hired another company to redo the stream. While she kept the original watercourse, the eye-jarring concrete lining was jackhammered up and replaced with a more deeply laid plastic liner hidden by various kinds of rock. Parts of the stream are now 60 centimetres deep to accommodate the roots of hardy waterlilies. Large underwater rocks conceal pumps that circulate the water, and plants set out on ledges look as if they sprouted there naturally. To create bogs along the banks, she laid a soaker hose 75 centimetres under the surface alongside a liner punctured here and there to allow the water to drain away slowly.

She likes the look she achieved: "Lush

The reflexing petals of the martagon lily, above centre, add drama to the summer garden, and globeflower, above, is one of the yellows that repeats through the garden. The annual poppies at right seed with abandon in the backlane garden. In fall the garden boasts rich colour in the yellow of fading hostas, red leaves and creamy hydrangea puffs.

and full, with a variety of textures and something different happening every season." The trees define the structure without overwhelming the yard. The lacy foliage of the little-leafed lindens and the narrow needles of the Scotch pines form an open canopy, unlike the dense wall created by the spruce that's more common to Edmonton.

Joan didn't spend a lot of time plotting her garden on paper. "I'm spontaneous. If I like a plant, I buy it and then decide where it will go. If it's wrong, I move it. Don't beat yourself up about mistakes."

Neither does she entirely blame professionals for creating cookie-cutter yards. Landscapers often are not plantsmen, and they're limited to the selection offered by local nurseries. But gardeners aren't, she points out. She shops out of catalogues from all over North America. Different isn't necessarily difficult. "Peonies grow well here, so grow peonies. But not the same varieties everybody does. There are hundreds of varieties." Joan also isn't wedded to what is supposed to grow in her Zone 3 area. Despite extreme low temperatures, Edmonton generally has continuous snowcover that protects plants in winter. Joan shovels extra snow onto some, such as rhododendrons, that are borderline hardy. She doesn't cut down plants in the fall, allowing the dead foliage to become

an added layer of insulation. Only a few of her plants, such as tree peonies, David Austin roses and butterfly bush (*Buddleia davidii*) require coddling in the Edmonton climate. These shrubs, untrimmed except for some light pruning of the roses, go under plastic garbage cans with the bottoms removed, into which she stuffs shredded leaves and peat moss.

Joan finds solace in her garden. She spends a couple of hours there every evening after work. "In a week's time I weed through every bed. It's so restful, relaxing. You get what I call good-tired: a hot bath, a glass of red wine and I sleep well."

It's her mission, she feels, to spread the gardening message: "Don't be afraid to try something new. There's a ton of stuff out there. Let loose a little." ■

plantsfor
fourseasons

Landscape architect Neil Turnbull grows some six hundred species of trees at his farm near Sunderland, Ontario. "Evergreen and deciduous shrubs offer size, texture and dynamics to a garden year-round," he says. Berries, shapely stems, trunks with peeling bark and branches with unusual forms add colour and character, as do plants that retain their leaves or flowers. Try to select plants with a wide range of desirable attributes. ■

TEN PLANT PICKS:
CLIMBING HYDRANGEA
    (*Hydrangea anomala petiolaris* spp.) Zone 5
EUROPEAN BEECH
    (*Fagus sylvatica*—various cultivars) Zone 4
DAWN REDWOOD
    (*Metasequoia glyptostroboides*) Zone 4
NOOTKA WEEPING CYPRESS
    (*Chamaecyparis nootkatensis* 'Pendula') Zone 4
SERBIAN SPRUCE
    (*Picea omorika*) Zone 4
DWARF ALBERTA SPRUCE
    (*Picea glauca* 'Conica') Zones 2 to 6
PAPERBARK MAPLE
    (*Acer griseum*) Zone 4
STRIPED MAPLE
    (*Acer pensylvanicum*) Zone 3
BAYBERRY
    (*Myrica pensylvanica*) Zones 2 to 6
SNOWBERRY
    (*Symphoricarpos albus*) Zone 3

Nootka weeping cypress

Bayberry

Snowberry

Beech

Paperbark maple

Striped maple

theroot of goodgardening

For soils with low or high pH levels, choose plants with a preference for acidity or alkalinity. Here are some suggestions:

ACID-TOLERANT
Fir trees
Cedar
Oaks
Pines
Mountain laurel
   (*Kalmia* spp.)
Rhododendrons
Yews
Azaleas
Heathers (*Calluna* spp.)
Chrysanthemums
Lily-of-the-valley
Heaths (*Erica* spp.)
Lilies
Cardinal flower
   (*Lobelia cardinalis*)
Lupines
Fennel
Potatoes
Radishes
Rhubarb
Blackberries
Blueberries
Raspberries

ALKALINE-TOLERANT
Sweet clover
Maple trees
Hawthorns
Kentucky coffee tree
Carnations (*Dianthus* spp.)
Baby's-breath
Irises
Sweet peas
Phlox
Nasturtiums
Asparagus
Beets
Cauliflower
Leeks
Lettuce
Onions
Parsnips
Spinach
Swiss chard

The matter of soil pH—the measurement of soil alkalinity and acidity—bedevils gardeners. Which is the best to have? How does pH affect plant growth and how can it be changed or influenced?

Let's start with an understanding of what determines the alkaline or acidic character of soil. Dig a hole deep enough and you'll strike bedrock—the most influential factor. If acidic rock, such as granite, is under your soil, frost action will distribute tiny particles of rock minerals through the soil and turn the pH toward acidity. Conversely, an alkaline rock such as limestone will push soil pH toward alkalinity.

Just about anything can be measured on the pH scale, which runs from 0 to 14, with the middle point of 7 being neutral. Ratings below 7 are acidic, while ratings above 7 are alkaline. The term pH means "parts hydrogen," and refers to the concentration of positively charged hydrogen ions in a soil sample. Hydrogen ions are electrically charged atoms that determine soil fertility and are most active (meaning they rapidly attach mineral molecules to themselves) in soil with slightly acid 6.5 to neutral 7 ratings. At lower and higher pH levels, the hydrogen ions become negatively charged and are therefore less active.

Most plants grow best in soil with a pH of 6.5. to 7. Below 5 (very acidic) or above 8 (very alkaline), the availability of nutrients is affected, and plants grow poorly. Calcium, magnesium and potassium are insoluble in soil below 5 and can't be absorbed by plant roots. Similarly, phosphorus is insoluble in soil above 8.

Soil-testing services can accurately measure pH from a small sample. Home-testing kits and inexpensive meters can determine if a soil is acidic or alkaline but they won't give an accurate pH reading.

If soil is acidic, its pH can be temporarily raised with the addition of 10 to 12 kilograms of dolomite lime per 9 square metres. If soil is alkaline, adding sulfur at a ratio of 5 to 7.5 kilograms per 9 square metres will temporarily lower pH by one unit. But the natural pH character of your soil is likely to return to normal within 6 to 12 months.

Another way to cope with low or high pH levels is to grow plants with a preference for acidity or alkalinity. However, adding generous amounts of organic material to low or high pH soils will effectively buffer extreme pH conditions and help all plants to grow better.

HOW TO TAKE A SOIL SAMPLE
Take three small samples from different areas of your garden.

For each sample, dig a wedge-shaped hole 15 centimetres deep and set the soil aside. Remove a 2.5-centimetre slice of soil from the full depth all the way down one side of the hole.

Combine the three soil slices to get a representative sample. Spread the mixture out to air dry on several sheets of clean paper. When dry, collect approximately 250 mL of soil in a plastic container for submission to a testing facility.

To find a soil-testing facility in your area, check **www.canadiangardening.com/ html/cg_soiltesting.html**. ∎

year-round garden

Well-placed plantings hold their own all year round, especially with a blanket of snow. Beautiful gates are more noticeable in winter, with fine details such as crosspieces and trellis-work that become shelves for snow or make patterns in the pale sunlight. And don't throw out old garden furniture—worn willow or Muskoka chairs make fine sculptures.

Landscape designers don't depend on plants alone to create a garden with year-round interest. The overall plan of the garden, the garden's architecture and accessories—what many designers like to call its "bones"— play an important role, especially in winter. Here are some guidelines to keep in mind when you're planning for all-season interest in your garden, from Toronto landscape designer Penny Arthurs.

• Subdivide. Break up spaces to create different moods and service different functions: sitting, dining, storage, play.

• Screen out problem views. Use a light touch and a feeling of transparency rather than drawing attention to what you're trying to hide.

• Treat plants as living architecture or building blocks. Consider foliage, form, bloom period, berries, branching structure. In a small garden, each plant must pay its way.

• Pare down the palette. Cut down the elements at play: introduce a few bold furnishings—10 of one plant rather than several different species.

• Create focal points. Use garden furnishings and ornaments

as "magnets and punctuations" that draw you to certain spots or lure the eye to other views.

• Define and decorate. Consider both the form and function of essential elements. Pathways direct the route through a garden and add ground-level texture and pattern. Steps, gates and fences offer other possibilities. ▪

Relax, play games and entertain in gardens designed for living

family gardens

134 BLURRING THE LINES

140 PARTY GARDEN

146 THINKING BIG

152 COTTAGE IN THE CITY

FAMILY PROJECTS
160 GROWING UP GARDENING

PLANT SOLUTIONS
168 PLANTS FOR PATHWAYS

blurring
thelines

GARDEN ROOMS BLEND WITH THE HOUSE IN AN EDMONTON OASIS
BY MARILYNN McARA

Susan Roberts and Jiri Novak didn't
need to find a suitable place to hold their
wedding ceremony and reception: it was
right in Susan's own backyard. For Susan,
who has a flair for design and a passion for
gardening, it was a particular joy to celebrate
with friends and family in a space she had
designed herself. And for both Susan and
Jiri, some of the most lasting visual memories of their 1996 wedding—lush bouquets
of russet-coloured roses and pepperberries,
peony petals scattered on woodchip paths,

charming decorative groupings of colourful
birdhouses—are inextricably woven into
their evolving garden.

The garden, a carefully planned series of
"rooms," is a true extension of the house,
flowing naturally from it by means of similar construction materials and colour
schemes, and transitional areas such as the
7.5-metre-long greenhouse room on the
south side of the house. Windows give the
living room and dining room a direct visual
connection with the garden, and a covered
porch at the back of the house provides great
views of the garden. A large fire pit in the
garden is used by family and friends for barbecues even in winter. Beyond that is a herb
garden, its brick edging almost hidden by
the closely planted dill, mint, chamomile,
French tarragon, chives and basil. There's a
potting area; a play area that Susan's son,

The pond is set amidst a bed of perennials adjoining the firepit area, which is used even in winter for cook-outs, and it's a focus of the garden. The cool green hosta leaves contrast with the deep blue of a birdbath, a deliberate combination created by a colour-sensitive gardener.

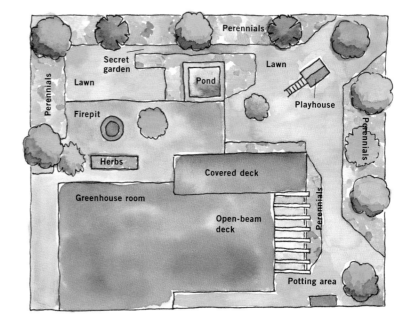

Reid, used when he was younger, which includes a playhouse and a patch of lawn big enough for playing catch; and a natural pond filled with goldfish and water plants. And near the rear boundary of the lot is a shady pathway—Reid calls it the secret garden— overhung by the branches of native poplars, mountain ash (*Sorbus americana*) and a bur oak (*Quercus macrocarpa*). The pathway is made even more secluded by honeysuckle, ivy and clematis that have outgrown

their twig arbours at either end and reach into the tree branches.

Susan wasn't always an avid gardener, but her attitude changed when the dream home she'd designed was finished and she realized the lot was bare. "So I learned how to grow my own plants," she says. "It was really by trial and error. I'd order seeds from places like Australia; things that didn't have a hope of surviving here, and of course they all died. But gradually I learned." She now grows up to eight thousand annuals and perennials from seed each year.

Right from the beginning, the garden's design was carefully thought out. "I like straight, clean lines," Susan says. "But to soften the garden, the plantings are all

Susan has a strong sense of design and colour, and although she likes the discipline of straight lines, she softens the overall plan with loose flower beds that include bright orange Oriental poppies, perennial geraniums, dianthus, delphiniums, columbine and shasta daisies. At the rear of the garden is a shady secret pathway, above, hidden by native poplars, bur oak and mountain ash and entered via twig arbours.

creating transitions

Susan Roberts' garden was designed to be an integral part of her family's living quarters. "There are no definite lines or barriers," she says. "There's a natural flow from indoors to outdoors, and vice versa."

Pivotal in the transition is the greenhouse room: in winter its thousands of seedlings and tropicals provide a preview of next summer's garden; in summer its windows allow a protected view of the garden.

The textures of construction materials also create a sense of transition. "There's a progression from wood to stone to grass to dirt," Susan says. The smooth, hardwood floors in the house, for example, flow into the plank flooring of the indoor greenhouse room and adjacent porch; from there, a patio and paths, both made of stone, progress to lawn, the pond and a wood-chip path into the secluded pathway of the secret garden. The shift in materials is also evident in the furniture: more formal indoors, it gradually becomes less formal in the kitchen, on the porch, with its wrought-iron-and-glass table and chairs in bold print, and at the firepit, which is surrounded by rustic cedar lounge chairs.

A subtle indoor/outdoor transition is felt in the degree of protection from the elements as one goes through sliding doors to the covered part of the porch, seen next page, then to an uncovered part, the patio and the garden.

The natural flow is aided by repeating details such as the tongue-and-groove cedar used for ceilings in the covered porch and the adjacent indoor greenhouse room; the brick support columns in the covered porch that echo the interior use of brick in the fireplaces and the walls of the greenhouse room; and natural materials (twigs, greenery, flowers) used as decoration both inside and out. The colour schemes are also repeated: black and white in the kitchen and adjacent covered porch; white furniture and walls in the second-floor loft and an adjoining upper deck.

Susan Roberts' garden is a conscious extension of the family's home. A wraparound porch with a covered dining area is liveable in rainy summer weather, and the greenhouse room offers a warm winter refuge. Susan planned the garden as a series of rooms, including a play area, for family activities.

very wild, very tangled. I don't want it to look too manicured." Waves of colour are provided throughout the garden by perennials such as columbine, shasta daisies, Oriental poppies, lupines, salvia, brown-eyed Susan, lambs'-ears, delphiniums and dianthus. Peonies are a particular favourite: there are five in the perennial garden by the pond, and several more in the cutting garden on the west side of the lot. "I chose early-, mid- and late-season varieties so I have blooms as long as possible," she says.

Another important requirement was leaving enough space for Reid and

Buckshot, their golden retriever. "They needed room to play, so that's why I incorporated patches of lawn and the playhouse."

In the garden's continuing evolution, Jiri has helped her create new areas such as the enlarged beds on the west of the property. "We're always changing what we plant there," Susan says, "but this year we have a vegetable patch and cutting garden, as well as some hardy Morden roses. They like the hot sun against the west wall." Jiri also takes care of all the trees and does the pruning. It's Reid's responsibility to look after the pond in the back garden and the half-barrel pond in the front courtyard. Early in the morning on one of the first days of summer each year, he and his mother set off for the countryside outside Edmonton

to re-stock the ponds. Accompanied by Buckshot, they collect plants such as water crowfoot (*Ranunculus aquatilis*), marsh marigold (*Caltha palustris*) and Labrador tea (*Ledum groenlandicum*), as well as mud rich with nutrients, snails and frogs' eggs. Reid is always eager to show off his pond to friends, and he enjoys feeding the goldfish, which overwinter in his uncle's aquarium.

As for Susan, whether she's sitting on the covered deck reading with Buckshot snoozing beside her, or relaxing with her family and friends around the firepit, there's no place like home—and that most definitely includes her garden. ▪

partygarden

GARDENING COMES FIRST, BUT ENTERTAINING IS A STRONG SECOND
BY KATHY VEY

Sunny and Peter Montgomery think nothing of inviting a hundred people over for a potluck dinner on their large and inviting deck, which nearly fills the back garden and is surrounded by dense plantings of porcelain vine, silver-lace and hydrangea. At night it's lit by several candelabra. Right: 'Graham Thomas' rose

It seems only natural that someone named Sunny would live in a community called the Beach. The boardwalk stretch of parkland where Toronto's east end meets the shore of Lake Ontario makes up only a small part of the neighbourhood; most of the streets, including the one where Sunny Montgomery lives with her husband, Peter, slope upward into a leafy patchwork of converted cottages, modest semi-detached homes, half-finished renos and spanking-new houses. In the summer, if you cock

your head just so, you might discern the roar of a distant Jet Ski over the rumble of streetcars trundling past the seemingly countless cafés of Queen Street East.

Less than half a block from the hubbub of this commercial spine is the Montgomerys' house, a dwelling they've transformed in the seven years since they moved in. At that time, thanks to the ministrations of a care-taking neighbour, the front yard was a wall-to-wall carpet of green—"the best grass on the street," Sunny admits. What she doesn't mention is that not a blade of the stuff remains. There's no room for it.

At curbside, a pair of standard-trained Arctic willows (*Salix arctica*) reach out tendrils of dusky leaves toward passersby. Locked in an embrace with a tangle of clematis, the shrubs flank a set of rustic—and rusty—iron gates that swing inward to

a tumult of colour and foliage on either side of an inviting red flagstone walkway. Densely planted and underplanted, the front garden bursts out of its borders with a kaleidoscope of trumpet lilies, roses in every shade, fragrant thymes underfoot among the pavers, and knock-out fronds of butterfly bush aspiring to give visitors a poke in the eye. A dual-coloured 'Shirobana' spirea (*Spiraea japonica* 'Shirobana') daintily jostles for space with a cut-leaf Japanese maple (*Acer palmatum* 'Garnet').

Somewhere in all this glory you'll find Sunny, either hard at work or lost in thought, possibly parked in one of the giddily blue-painted Muskoka chairs that rest at the foot of the broad, equally blue, front steps. A cat or two—Diego, the Himalayan, who's shamelessly affection-ate, and old, grey Sandino—will hover nearby, waiting for attention.

"I sit and I stare," explains Sunny. "I'm what you would call a haphazard garden-er, not a planner."

She was a stranger to gardening when she and Peter moved to the house in 1994. "The thought of putting my hands in dirt?" she asks in mock horror, recall-ing the bumper crop of weeds "as tall as that tree" that greeted the couple in the backyard.

To her surprise, puttering in the soil felt really good. She began by taking out the grass in the front garden, putting in a ton of peat moss and manure, and then planting whatever took her fancy. "Everything planted the first year just took off like crazy," says Sunny.

That winter she started reading every-thing she could get her mitts on. "I plant-ed delphiniums the first year, peonies the next year. At the end of the summer, I yanked 'em out. Later I found out they were perennials," she says, laughing.

Serendipity played as much of a role as trial and error in the evolution of the gar-den on their 9-metre by 38-metre lot. When inspiration struck, she sketched ideas on paper napkins, cajoled reluctant contractors and lobbied her husband, himself a renovator. What developed was an English cottage–style planting with a slightly loco south-of-the-border feel. Curvy clay pots lounge at the base of a robust patch of phlox, while a Mexican

Sunny prefers flowers to foliage and colour over texture, but her garden has a balance of both, as can be seen in the small front-yard pond, where a cutleaf Japanese maple contrasts with the ripply leaves of hosta. Right: the deck has a quiet corner as well as a place to dine. Far left: 'Sexy Rexy' rose

chiminea perches by the front doors.

Long before she discovered her zest for gardening, Sunny—and yes, that is her given name—fell in love with Latino culture. While still a teenager in small-town Peterborough, Ontario, she made a high school trip to Spain; she followed that with extensive travel through El Salvador (she lived there for four months), Guatemala and Mexico in the 1970s, and countless trips to the American Southwest with her husband.

These days, as the regional director for Canada of the Puerto Rican Tourism Company, a government agency, she travels frequently to the Caribbean—which, sadly, doesn't leave her much time for gardening. "I've been known to take a week of holidays to plant in spring, and just spend it in kneepads," she says. The results of her labour are out front for all to see and appreciate—the neighbour-

hood is a bastion for the old-fashioned practice of sitting on the verandah and keeping an eye on the Joneses.

As for the Montgomerys, despite the effort that went into their front garden, they make equal use of their backyard, a space recently transformed to indulge their love of entertaining. They think nothing of hosting a sister's wedding or inviting a hundred friends over for a potluck dinner during the annual summer jazz and street festival.

A massive, knotty Western red cedar deck, built two summers ago, stretches from the back doors nearly to the fence line. "It smells heavenly when it's wet. It's like being transported to a forest after it rains," Sunny says. Peter nods in agreement: "We don't need a cottage."

In fact, the deck has a touch of dock about it. Whimsical posts, a second-hand-store find, joined by a hefty length of rope, delineate the edge of the raised

deck near the garage, lest any partygoer topple overboard into the hostas after one too many glasses of sangria. (Actually, the garage is in disguise, sporting a thick cloak of Virginia creeper during the warm-weather months.)

Just try counting the intoxicating colours within eyeshot: cobalt and turquoise berries cluster like gemstones on a porcelain vine (*Ampelopsis brevipedunculata*) scrambling up the fence; mop-headed big-leaf hydrangeas (*H. macrophylla*), some pink, some blue, flounce nearby. Here's a silver-lace vine shimmering in a shady corner, and there's a purple-leaf plum tree and a standard-trained Siberian dogwood (*Cornus alba* 'Sibirica'). The back fence is draped with clematis and an elegant French lilac ('Mme. Lemoine').

"Oh, look at this one—it's a 'Bonica' rose, my favourite. It didn't get watered for a year while the deck was being built and it was sitting in pure sand. I looked out here one day and it had 12 buds on one stem." She shakes her head at the luck of it all, the *que sera* nature of her garden. "I just put these guys in and they grow," she smiles. "Everyone's really happy out here."

Especially Sunny. ∎

The Montgomerys' front garden, once a patch of the best grass in the neighbourhood, is now a welcoming beacon on their street, tumbling with flowers and warm colour. It has a south-west feeling despite the early-Toronto iron gate and cottage-style paving. Below: one of many daylily cultivars in the garden

thinkingbig

SOME LARGER–THAN–LIFE ADVICE FOR A SMALL FAMILY GARDEN
BY PAMELA YOUNG

The owners needed play space for their small children and an area for big family dinners. And they'd inherited an unattractive but imposing hot tub. On top of it all, they weren't gardeners. What to do? Call in an empathetic designer, who created a low-maintenance garden of rooms.

When a client asked Arthurs to design a garden for their family behind their big, Georgian-style home in North Toronto, she had a rectangle of fairly modest proportions—approximately 12 metres to the back fence and 18 metres from side to side—to work with. Jutting into the space was a sizable, squarish family room that had been recently added to the back of the house.

Apart from a few shrubs planted around the perimeter and a hot tub near the house, the yard was a flat, blank slate. The owners were hoping Arthurs could make the tight site perform a variety of functions. Because they have a large extended family, they wanted an al fresco dining area to accommodate a pretty big crowd. They also required play space for their two young children. And they wanted to be able to look out their back windows all summer and see a profusion

The house is large; the lot is not. So how do you make a garden used by an active family seem more spacious than it is?

Many people's first impulse would be to go for an unbroken expanse of lawn edged with plantings. But experience has taught landscape designer Penny Arthurs, of the Toronto firm The Chelsea Gardener, that first impulses can be dead wrong. As she says, "The more intensive and varied the use of a space, the larger it looks."

The challenge was to divide the relatively small space behind a big house so it appeared larger. To do this, designer Penny Arthurs built a ground-level terrace across the back of the house and created three distinct areas leading away from it: a tree-lined pathway, the central rose garden and an open lawn for play. The hot tub was the hard part, but putting it into its own little room solved the problem.

of flowers—many that could be cut for bouquets.

The central challenge, as Arthurs saw it, was to divide the lot in ways that would expand the sense of space. "I tried to give a sense of pushing back the boundaries of the garden so they don't seem to be crowding the house," she says.

Arthurs got rid of all the inherited landscape elements except the hot tub, and she performed two sleights-of-hand that savvy garden designers have relied on for centuries. First, she created a ground-level stone terrace flush with the back of the house: it encases the house and is contained by a low brick wall that serves as a perch during those large family gatherings. Second, in the garden, Arthurs created strong axes in pathways and plantings leading toward the back fence. These geometric lines pull your eye away from the house and make the yard look deeper. Meandering lines would not have produced the same illusion of depth. At the end of the garden, the paths connect to form a route around the garden. "When there's a route, you're able to do a lot more in the space, and you can see all the plantings from different angles," Arthurs says.

If you stand on the terrace facing the garden, you see three distinct areas—or "rooms," as Arthurs calls them. On the right is a straight pathway that reaches deep into the back corner of the lot. Between the fence and the brick-accented sandstone squares of the path grow columnar crabapples underplanted with sweet woodruff (*Galium odoratum*) and white spring-flowering bulbs. On the other side of the path is a shrub border of dogwoods, dwarf lilacs and hydrangeas. "The object is to intensify your use of the space, in addition to thrusting the lines away from the house," says Arthurs. "And by taking the pathway right to the boundary, you make use of space that would otherwise go unused."

Close to the back fence, the path takes a 90° turn and leads into the central "room"—a formal rose garden symmetrically laid out around a circular bed with a tall wrought-iron obelisk at its centre. The rose garden may also be entered from the terrace off the family room of the house.

To the left of the rose garden is the sunken lawn that is a favourite play space. Although the lawn is just one step down from the rest of the garden, the subtle grade change makes the entire yard seem more spacious—and look more interesting. As well, the owners said they'd need space for special occasions such as First Communions and weddings, and wanted an area large enough to set up a marquee.

The fourth outdoor room was the trickiest. Before Arthurs came on the scene, the large hot tub dominated the rather barren yard—and hot tubs just aren't natural beauties. Arthurs was also stuck with its crudely faced stone sides. She made it blend in by using the same Credit Valley sandstone she used on the terrace and the paths to cap the tub's exterior walls.

Because the tub is in a sunny part of the garden, Arthurs decided to make it the focal point of a Mediterranean-style area. A couple of large planters screen the tub and she designed an elegant, lattice-front storage shed ("I prefer to call it a garden house," she says with a laugh)

for this area. "In the old garden, the tub seemed much bigger and more prominent because it was all there was in the space. Now we've put it away in its own little room. It dominates that room rather than the whole garden."

The owners of this garden rely on a maintenance person to keep their greenery in impeccable Georgian order. "Because they aren't gardeners, it gave me an opportunity to choose a more limited palette of plant material than plant collectors will allow," Arthurs says. "From my point of view as a designer, a limited palette is a good thing. People usually want too many different plants. Here, I was able to do some bold planting, such as the columnar crabapples along the long walk. Along the back are flowering dogwoods (*Cornus kousa*), which have an architectural quality. I like to be able to use more than one of them."

Arthurs chose simple plants for most of the garden. The only area with a mix of perennials and shrubs is the border between the rose garden and the lawn. It includes yarrow, cotoneaster and tree peony. For the rose garden, Arthurs chose varieties with star quality—but not star temperament. They bloom all summer and are so prolific the bushes don't look denuded when flowers are clipped

for floral arrangements. The white roses are 'Iceberg'; the small, pale pink shrubs are 'Bonica'; and the deeper pink, 'Morden's Blush'. 'New Dawn', another pink, climbs the central obelisk.

The only annuals in the garden grow in the containers in the hot tub area and atop the seating wall. The containers themselves are noteworthy for the boldness of their scale. Their massiveness reflects yet another of Arthurs' strategies for making the space appear bigger. "I think it's important to keep the scale large in a small garden," she says. "The smaller things are, the fussier they feel."

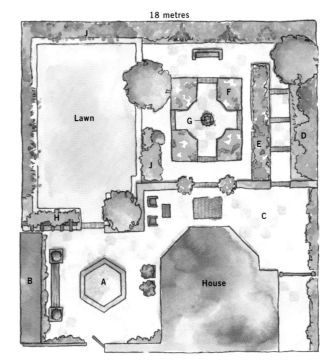

18 metres

A Hot tub
B Garden house
C Terrace
D Crabapples, spring bulbs
E Dogwood, lilac, hydrangea
F Roses
G Obelisk
H Arbour
J Perennial border

creatingunity

Although landscape designer Penny Arthurs divided this Toronto garden into "rooms," each with a distinct character, she also wanted the space to be a unified whole. Continuity of materials pulls the design together: Credit Valley sandstone, red-brick accents and fencing finished with an opaque exterior stain Arthurs calls "greige"—a colour halfway between grey and beige.

By capping the hot-tub walls with the same sandstone slabs she used for the paths and to top the brick seating wall, Arthurs was able to blend in a cumbersome existing feature. Meanwhile, the terra-cotta brick, also used as banding in the sandstone paving, matches the house brick and ties the entire garden to the residence.

Many of the brick bands set into the paving mark the boundaries between different rooms of the formal garden. On the terrace between the family room's French doors and the rose garden, Arthurs inset a brick "welcome mat" (visible in the photo at right)—a device, she says, sometimes used in the gardens of Renaissance Italy. "It adds interest and breaks up a large expanse of stone, but it's also a welcoming transition between one space and another."

One of the challenges was to unify the wood fencing—on one side it was new, on two sides older, and all were different. Staining everything the same neutral shade helped give the sense of one treatment. Arthurs also used the same stain on new benches, planters and the latticed garden house near the hot tub. "Unless you get a very high-quality and extremely expensive clear cedar, you get a lot of irregularities in the wood," she says. "By staining it, you get a clean, coherent look."

cottagein thecity

A SHADY GARDEN BRINGS BACK MEMORIES OF SUMMERS AT THE LAKE
BY PAMELA YOUNG

Cathy Jones admits they bought their old Toronto house because of an ancient maple tree on the property, but life under its shady branches has made the choice worthwhile. The summer house and the *boules* court they built at the end of the garden add to their garden's vacation mood.

When Cathy Jones gazes out her kitchen window, what she sees looks a lot like Ontario cottage country and a little like France. In reality, Cathy and her husband, David Reville, live in east-central Toronto, just across the leafy Don Valley from the urban core. But happy memories of a family cottage, and the presence of an immense old silver maple at the foot of their property, inspired Cathy and David to create the appearance of wilderness in their own backyard.

Native plants and a pavilion reminiscent of the sleeping porch of an old-fashioned cottage bring a north-country look to this plot of land in the big city. In front of the cottage stoop is the Gallic element: a sand-filled clearing for playing *boules*, a French bowling game. Along with all the other elements that make up the property, including three small terraces and the rambling garden of perennials and roses closer to the house, it adds variety and informality to a landscape that delights everyone, from Cathy and David to their young granddaughter, Marley, a frequent visitor.

Cathy confesses that the big maple tree—estimated by an arbourist to be between 125 and 150 years old—was what made them decide to buy the property two decades ago. "Up to that point, we were being totally sensible—we'd looked at many other places

cottagein thecity

A SHADY GARDEN BRINGS BACK MEMORIES OF SUMMERS AT THE LAKE
BY PAMELA YOUNG

Cathy Jones admits they bought their old Toronto house because of an ancient maple tree on the property, but life under its shady branches has made the choice worthwhile. The summer house and the *boules* court they built at the end of the garden add to their garden's vacation mood.

When Cathy Jones gazes out her kitchen window, what she sees looks a lot like Ontario cottage country and a little like France. In reality, Cathy and her husband, David Reville, live in east-central Toronto, just across the leafy Don Valley from the urban core. But happy memories of a family cottage, and the presence of an immense old silver maple at the foot of their property, inspired Cathy and David to create the appearance of wilderness in their own backyard.

Native plants and a pavilion reminiscent of the sleeping porch of an old-fashioned cottage bring a north-country look to this plot of land in the big city. In front of the cottage stoop is the Gallic element: a sand-filled clearing for playing *boules*, a French bowling game. Along with all the other elements that make up the property, including three small terraces and the rambling garden of perennials and roses closer to the house, it adds variety and informality to a landscape that delights everyone, from Cathy and David to their young grand-daughter, Marley, a frequent visitor.

Cathy confesses that the big maple tree—estimated by an arbourist to be between 125 and 150 years old—was what made them decide to buy the property two decades ago. "Up to that point, we were being totally sensible—we'd looked at many other places

The *boules* court, seen below, takes up precious planting room, but Cathy is pleased with the open space it leaves in the otherwise dense garden. The white cast-iron garden furniture once belonged to Cathy's mother-in-law. Plants like the orange daylilies and pink Asiatic lily, seen on the opening page and below, and *Fritillaria meleagris*, opposite, are in keeping with the cottage theme.

and checked out the plumbing and the wiring," she says. "Then I walked into this backyard and saw the tree and thought, 'I love this.' We made a totally illogical decision based on the tree."

The house, built early in the 20th century, is a gable-roofed, porch-fronted red-brick structure, linked to the sidewalk by a steep flight of stairs. By the time Cathy and David bought it, its years of use as a rooming house had left it in sorry repair. "It was a wreck," Cathy says.

Fixing up the house was the first priority. But even in the early years, Cathy—the daughter of avid gardeners—made

time to plant things out back. "At first I planted vegetables, ignoring the fact that you need a lot of sun for vegetables, and this is mostly a shade garden," she says. "Later, I started buying perennials because they were investment plants—they got bigger."

Many of the present perennials came her way when friends and family members made divisions. A couple of plantings of Solomon's-seal grew from two stems given to Cathy 15 years ago. The

snowdrops that now cover much of her garden in early spring were propagated from a small clump from her parents' garden. And she can't bear to part with two summer phloxes from her childhood home, even though they're not new mildew-resistant hybrids.

In the 1980s, Cathy fulfilled a lifelong dream and attended art school, and as a gardener who also happens to be an artist she's keenly interested in composition. Because the area is four times longer than it is wide—approximately 24 metres by 6 metres—she organized her garden into a chain of "rooms" between the back of the house and the cottage-style pavilion at the foot of the property. The land formerly sloped gently down toward the back of the lot, but Cathy had it regraded into a series of terraces. Some of these, such as the flagstone terrace that's a single step down from the main flower garden, are only a few feet in length, but each successive element enriches the whole. Meals are often taken on the flagstone terrace just outside the back door; a potting bench is tucked into a nook hidden from the table. A walk around an arbour on the same level leads to the main perennial border. From there, you step down to a short terrace, with a cast-iron Victorian bench and chairs, that overlooks the

boules court. At another, slightly different level, a flagstone path between two gardens leads to the garage and cottage porch. Grass paths connect the first and second terrace, and wind around the arbour and perennial border.

Years ago, a French friend introduced Cathy and David to the game of *boules*. They enjoyed it so much that they decided to create a *boules* court in their own garden. The court, near the back of the property, is an expanse of sand about 6 metres long and 5 metres across at its widest point. "It was a big amount of grief to give up that amount of garden space," Cathy says, "but in the end I'm really pleased with the open space. I like the way the negative space, the quiet space, sets up the other areas." However, she and David felt that too much of the *boules* court was visible from the pavilion at the back of the garden, so David constructed a woodpile that partially screens the view of the playing surface.

The one-room pavilion that terminates the sequence of spaces is Cathy's tribute to past cottages. "When we built this, the family cottage had been sold," she says. "We didn't want to have a cottage ourselves, but I was nostalgic for the sleeping porch—a place to come out to in the morning and have your coffee." With the help of a friend who is a set designer, Cathy designed a 2.5 metre by 3.5 metre wooden structure that looks just like an old cottage porch and even sounds like one: its screen door opens with a squeak and closes with a satisfying thunk. Inside the cozy retreat are book-filled shelves, comfortably shabby chairs and a cot for afternoon siestas. In the cold months, it serves as a storage shed for garden furniture.

The plants in this part of the garden are in keeping with the cottage theme; most are native, even local. Her pride and joy is the oakleaf hydrangea

(*Hydrangea quercifolia*), which has long-lasting, creamy-white blooms in early July that deepen to a dusty pink in the latter part of the summer. Near it are Canadian hemlocks (*Tsuga canadensis*). Also in the area is a redbud (*Cercis canadensis*) that sulked for a long time, but recently agreed to grow for her. In the early spring, white trilliums (obtained through the Canadian Wildflower Society) put on an impressive display at the back of the garden. Periwinkle (*Vinca minor*) and sweet woodruff (*Galium odoratum*) are the main groundcovers in this spot, which also supports jack-in-the-pulpit (*Arisaema triphyllum*), false Solomon's-seal (*Smilacina racemosa*), hepatica, foamflower (*Tiarella cordifolia*) and wild ginger (*Asarum canadense*).

By leaving this part of the garden unwatered for 7 to 10 days, then soaking it with weeping hoses for three hours at a stretch, Cathy has trained her more established plants to develop the deeper root systems they need to become drought-resistant. To further reduce the need for watering, she mulches her garden with bark, compost and leaf mould in late spring. She makes some of the mulch; the rest, chiefly leaf mould from the city recycling depot, she buys.

Cathy used to swear she would never grow anything that would require substantial amounts of pesticides and fertilizers—but that was before she developed a passion for fussier-than-rugosa roses. In her upper garden, near the house, her half-dozen prize roses include the pale pink hybrid tea 'Dainty Bess' and the myrrh-scented pink-blend 'Constance Spry', a David Austin cultivar. These roses require mulch for winter protection, insecticidal soap for blackspot and

The summer house is a cozy spot for a nap or a good read and masquerades as a cottage in the woods. Around it bloom oakleaf hydrangea and daylilies. Above: white daffodils, *Tulipa tarda* Below: trillium

careful inspection for caterpillars.

Several years ago, Cathy took down the rusted old wire fence that surrounded their property and replaced it with a more substantial wooden one. However, she liked the look of the weathered, ripply wire so much, she turned part of the old fence into arbours for clematis and roses. She also attached fragments of the old fence to the new fence, where the

wire grids now act as trellises for climbing hydrangea, roses and clematis. Her favourite clematis varieties include 'Maidwell Hall', an early-blooming, shade-tolerant *Clematis macropetala* with blue, bell-shaped flowers, and a taller, pink-blossomed *C. montana* 'Grandiflora', which likes sun and blooms in May.

She has found that many popular plants don't do well in her shady, sandy garden. "It's a little damp and close," she says. Delphiniums couldn't hack it, but she considers her pink gas plant (*Dictamnus albus*) a wonderful delphinium substitute. This long-lived, slow-growing perennial hangs onto its leaves all year and blooms in early summer. Similarly, she has not had much luck with lavender, but her lavender stand-in, a *Caryopteris* shrub, is flourishing. One of her favourite recent additions to her upper garden is *Gaura lindheimeri*, a tall, slender perennial with fine, exotic-looking white blooms.

Recently, Cathy has found a new avenue of creative expression: designing other people's gardens. After she tackled a few projects for friends, word spread and she began to receive more commissions. While she continues to derive great pleasure from her own garden, she finds it stimulating to plan other people's spaces. As any artist knows, it's always exciting to begin work on a new canvas.

boules anyone?

In France, *boules* (also known as *pétanque*, and similar to *bocce*) is usually played on a rectangular, crushed-gravel surface about 13 metres long and 3 metres wide. However, Cathy (seen at right after a throw) and David have found that their irregularly shaped, sand-filled court is a perfectly acceptable facsimile.

Boules can be played one-on-one, or by two- or three-person teams. The person who has the first throw draws a circle in the sand at one end of the court. Standing within this circle, he or she throws a small, brightly coloured wooden ball (known as the pea, or *cochonnet*) at least 6 metres but no more than 11 metres, and then tosses a larger, chromium-covered steel ball (a *boule*) as close as possible to this target. From the same throwing circle, the other players then take turns attempting to toss their *boules* even closer to the coloured target. (Underhand, softball-style throws are frowned upon; boules should either be pitched overhand or rolled on the ground with the back of the hand leading the throw.)

No matter how many people participate, there are always 12 balls in play. After all 12 have been thrown, all *boules* from the team closer to the *cochonnet* than the closest *boule* from the other team each earn a point. The *boules* are marked with a distinguishing indented pattern for each team.

The game is played from end to end until one player (or team) attains a score of 13. The fanciest move possible is to drive another player's ball away from the target by dropping your *boule* directly on top of your opponent's, knocking it away, and replacing it with your own. "And if you want to be really authentic," Cathy advises, "you have to drink pastis, a licorice-flavoured apéritif, while you're playing." ◼

growingup gardening

Parents sometimes experience the joys of gardening alone, with grudging help from kids and teenagers who consider their time weeding or digging more than fair payment for the fun of playing with friends. But we'll wager that, armed with the projects that follow, any parent can lure a child into realizing that gardening, too, can be fun, as well as creative and rewarding. To spin on an old cliché, the family that creates together stays together.

The stacked pot shown at right contains a variety of succulents and annuals that withstand heat and sun: orange gazania, 'Daybreak' series; browallia 'Blue Bells'; sedums; stonecrop; hens-and-chickens; woolly thyme; and white creeping thyme.

STACKED CONTAINER

This simple, three-tiered planter can be built in an afternoon and makes an unusual container. The first step is to choose pots (terra-cotta or plastic ones are fine) in three sizes that allow enough space around each layer of pot for planting. Test for size at the garden centre by placing them inside one another; you'll need a gap of at least 10 centimetres between each pot (shown are 40-, 30- and 15-centimetre pots). And make sure they all have drainage holes so water doesn't back up in any of them.

Assemble the planter in its final resting place because the finished product may be heavy and awkward to move. Fill the largest pot with a planting mix to approximately 10 centimetres from the top. Centre the second-largest pot on the soil and gently wedge it in, just deep enough that it's stable and even.

To anchor the pots, use a bamboo, wood or metal stake that fits through the drainage holes—if it's too snug, the pots won't drain; too loose, and the planter will be unstable. To determine the length of the stake, measure the height of the base and middle planters, and then add about 8 centimetres. Push the stake through the drainage hole in the second-largest pot, through the mix in the base planter, and lodge it in the drainage hole of the base.

TIPS FOR CARE

• Select plants that spread and spill over the edges of the pots.
• Keep in mind that the top and middle pots may need watering more often than the bottom pot.
• Use pots that will overwinter without cracking.
• Replace bamboo or wood stakes annually if you need to. Check them for stability each spring before you start to plant.

Fill the middle pot with planting mix, and then place the drainage hole of the top pot over the stake and wedge the pot into the mix in the middle pot. Fill the top pot with mix, and then plant the three tiers. Because the planting area is limited, buy small plants in cell-packs rather than in large pots. (The exception is the top pot, which has more surface area.) There is plenty of room for root growth in the bottom and middle sections, however, so you can pack plants closely together. The final step is to water the planter thoroughly.

Plenty of plants will thrive in this planter. Try turning it into a miniature herb garden, or create a fountain effect using vines.

FUN WITH HYPERTUFA

Hypertufa containers are simple, cheap and high on charm. Made from Portland cement (pure, not pre-mixed, cement), peat moss and vermiculite, they're popular in England. According to people who have done it, making hypertufa is as easy as playing in the dirt. In short, hypertufa containers are fun for kids and parents to make together.

In England, the mix is traditionally shaped into rectangular troughs 60 centimetres to 90 centimetres long; but hypertufa can be fashioned into a dizzying number of sizes and shapes, from small, classic garden pots to large, flaring bowls. The pots are generally water- and weather-resistant, and the large sizes especially are less likely to crack or crumble during freezing than ceramic or terra-cotta pots. Still, it's a good idea to re-inforce hypertufa during construction with a fibremesh product—available at most concrete suppliers—for added strength.

Making a hypertufa container—from shaping it until it's ready to plant—takes about three weeks. The most time-consuming part is forming the container itself, which takes about an hour. From there, it's a matter of letting the hypertufa cure.

Hypertufa pots age well, taking on a slightly more weathered look through the years. If they crack (unlikely, if you add fibremesh), simply patch them with more hypertufa the next time you make a pot.

If you're making the containers in winter, you'll need a well-ventilated area, such as a basement or garage that can take a little mess and a little bit of barnyard smell while the pots cure.

The list of materials and directions here are for a rectangular trough 23 centimetres by 45 centimetres and 18 centimetres high, which is made in a plastic dishwashing basin.

MATERIALS

a wheelbarrow or other large container
   for mixing
rubber gloves
heavy plastic (garbage bags slit and
   opened are fine)
a mould (in addition to the
   dishwashing basin, possibilities
   include old pots, Styrofoam coolers
   and their lids, wooden boxes)
a sheet of plywood or other flat surface
   for a temporary base
17 litres of peat moss
17 litres of vermiculite
11 litres of Portland cement
1 cup/250 mL of fibremesh (optional)
13 litres of water
several short lengths of wooden dowels
   or sticks
a wire brush
a carpenter's file
a dust mask (optional, but useful if you
   have dust allergies)

1. Cover the mould tightly with plastic bags (you may omit this step if the mould is made of plastic) tucking in all the corners and taping the plastic into place. Or build the trough inside the form. This is even easier, but the exterior of the hypertufa will be smoother and less rustic-looking.

2. In a wheelbarrow, combine vermiculite, peat moss and Portland cement. Add a large handful of fibremesh if you're concerned about winter strength. Blend dry ingredients, add water and mix well with your hands (wearing rubber gloves). The blend should be thoroughly wet and the consistency of cottage cheese. You may halve this recipe for smaller projects.

3. Put the mould upside-down. Take handfuls of the mix and start at the bottom of the upside-down mould (which will be the

2

3

4

5

top of the hypertufa pot). Pat the mix into place, gently slapping as you work to remove air bubbles. You want the mixture to be 4 to 5 centimetres thick. Occasionally check the thickness with your finger or a stick and then smooth it back into place.

4. Working slowly and deliberately, build the pot from the bottom up, slapping to remove air bubbles and smoothing the surface as you build. If you're making the pot on the inside of a container (as in this photo), push and pat the mix firmly against the bottom and sides of the mould.

5. Once you reach the top of the mould (which will be the bottom of the pot), check the depth one last time before smoothing the surface with your hand. Then take a flat board and draw it firmly across the top so you have a flat bottom. You don't want the planted trough rocking in the garden. (This step is not necessary if you're building your pot inside the mould.)

6. Poke the dowels (or sticks) through the cement mixture to create drainage holes. You can leave the dowels in place and move

them every day or so (to make them easy to remove when the mixture is dry), or insert them at this point and then remove them.

7. Loosely cover the pot with plastic to help keep moisture from evaporating. Mist the pot occasionally the first few days to encourage even curing.

8. After a week, remove the plastic and let the planter sit, uncovered, for four to five more days.

9. Remove the pot from the mould by gently pulling on the plastic wrapped around the mould. The pots look heavy, but they are surprisingly light.

10. Once the plastic has been removed from the mould, smooth the edges of the trough with a carpenter's file. If it rocks, run the file over the bottom. If you want a more rustic look for a pot made inside the mould, use a wire brush to rough up the finish. Check drainage holes to make sure they're clear. If not, drill them out, or use a hammer and nail to clear them.

11. Spray the trough with a hose to remove lime that might have come to the surface, and let it cure for a few more weeks before planting.

6

7

MATERIALS

rubber gloves
heavy plastic sheeting
leaves
pre-mix concrete (one standard-
   size bag makes three leaves
   about 45 centimetres square
   and 8 centimetres thick)
mortar or cement colourant,
   if you want a colour other than
   light grey
chicken wire or 1-centimetre-
   square wire mesh
wire cutters

LEAF STEPPING STONES

These are easy to make out of concrete and offer another weekend project for families— or for one ambitious gardener who wants to create something different to lead the way to the compost bin. These stepping stones are not only attractive, they're strong enough to support an adult's weight but light enough to move, and they are able to withstand winter temperatures below -25°C.

Rhubarb leaves were used here to make the pattern, but any leaves with heavy, numerous veins, such as hostas or gunnera, would work. You can also shape round or square stepping stones and imprint with a pattern of leaves, such as lacy ferns or a branch of maple leaves.

Concrete is easy to work with. All you need is a tub or wheelbarrow for mixing the concrete powder with water, and a trowel, hoe or shovel to stir it. Be sure to clean tub and tools with a jet spray of water immediately after using, before the bits of leftover concrete dry in place.

1. Choose a level area that will remain undisturbed for several days. A driveway, concrete patio, bare patch of soil or even a patch of grass will work.

2. Cut a piece of plastic sheeting at least 15 centimetres larger all around than the leaf (or another desired shape), and place it on the ground. Put the leaf in the centre of the plastic, vein side up (photo 1).

3. Mix the concrete to a stiff consistency, following package instructions. Wearing rubber gloves or using a shovel, move concrete onto the leaf, spreading it almost to the edge of the leaf to a thickness of 2.5 to 4 centimetres; press firmly to eliminate air bubbles (photo 2). If you're using a small leaf or several leaves as a pattern in the stepping stone, spread the concrete to form the shape you want.

4. To ensure strength and durability, place chicken wire on the concrete to within 5 centimetres of the edge, overlapping pieces if necessary. Shovel concrete on top of the chicken wire (photo 3), again spreading to a thickness of 2.5 to 4 centimetres and pressing firmly to eliminate air bubbles.

5. Gently lift the plastic up around the design (photo 4), smooth edges with gloved hands or a trowel to ensure an even look, and place earth or gravel up around the form to support it while it cures.

6. Cover with a second piece of plastic to keep the concrete from drying out. Allow to cure for at least 48 hours, then lift the stepping stone from the plastic (the plastic peels away easily) and turn it over to see the walking surface.

7. Remove small pieces of vein or leaf with a hose turned to jet spray. If you've made the stepping stone in hot weather, much of the leaf will have already decomposed.

8. You can place the stones in the garden immediately, but avoid stepping on them until the concrete has completely cured— curing time depends on the type of concrete mix used, but it usually takes 5 to 7 days. Spray with water frequently during the curing period. Make sure the stones are set firmly in the ground so they won't move when walked on. ▪

1

2

3

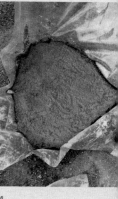

4

plantsfor pathways

A stroll down the garden path is more pleasant when the path is alive with plants. Splashes of foliage and tiny flowers peeping from between the stepping stones soften a path's hard edges and help integrate it into the garden. Buy small plants to begin with and gently tease them apart into the smallest sections possible in preparation for planting.

Paths are necessary in all gardens, especially in busy family gardens. They help divide areas of activity, as well as offering a safe and non-muddy route from the back door to the garbage bins. Stepping-stone paths made of random flagstone or concrete pavers are the easiest to install—and to change, once the sandbox is outgrown and removed in favour of an herb garden—and such paths look lovely surrounded or even overgrown by creeping plants.

Several companies now market entire lines of low-growing perennials specifically targeted for planting between stepping stones and pavers. A list of reliable plant choices begins on the next page.

plant solutions

Dig out small pockets where you want to plant and then add soil mixed with organic matter and a little coarse sand to support the roots. Use an old kitchen knife to tuck the tiny pieces of divided plants into the spaces. Water frequently for the first few months. Stones and pavers often create mini-microclimates that encourage quick growth.

Blue star creeper (*Isotoma fluviatilis*—formerly *Laurentia fluviatilis*) has small, oval, green leaves that are covered with star-shaped, light blue flowers in summer. A fast grower that's happy in sun or part shade, it needs regular watering and spreads 5 centimetres to 8 centimetres. Hardy to Zone 5 (worth growing as an annual in colder climates) and takes to light foot traffic.

Creeping Jenny/Moneywort (*Lysimachia nummularia*) spreads so rapidly that some consider it a weed. It thrives in persistently moist areas where other plants will not survive, but will also accept dry conditions. Its

bright yellow flowers bloom in midsummer and last for several weeks. Part sun or shade. *Lysimachia* 'Aurea' is a cultivar with yellow-green leaves. Moderate foot traffic. 5 centimetres. Zone 4.

Creeping speedwell (*Veronica repens*) is fast-growing and drought-tolerant, with small, shiny, green leaves and white or light lavender flowers in spring. A good choice for dark-coloured pavers, it actually thrives in heat and grows well in sun or part shade. 2.5 centimetres to 8 centimetres. Zone 4. *V. pectinata*, an extra-hardy alternative, has dense, deeply toothed, mat-like foliage and white-eyed, deep blue flowers. 5 centimetres to 8 centimetres. Zone 2.

Irish moss/Scotch moss (*Sagina subulata* and *S. subulata* 'Aurea') provides a lush cover of bright green (Irish) or golden-green (Scotch) highlighted with small, white flowers in late spring. Unlike true mosses, sagina performs well in sun as long as soil is kept moist. Regular footfalls won't bother it at all. 2.5 centimetres. Zone 4.

Labrador violet (*Viola labradorica*) has rounded green/blue/black leaves and small, purple flowers. Although it reseeds well, it serves best as an accent plant because its leaves are too dark for effective massed planting. Sun or part shade. 5 centimetres to 10 centimetres. Zone 2.

New Zealand brass buttons (*Cotula potentillina/Leptinella potentillina*) a creeper with hairy, fern-like, grey-green foliage tinged with bronze in fall and small, yellow, daisy-like flowers in spring and summer. Best in sun to part shade. Moderate foot traffic. 2 to 5 centimetres. Zone 5.

Rupturewort (*Herniaria glabra*) has tiny, tight, green leaves that turn bronze in winter. It prefers sun but tolerates part shade as well, and straying feet. Annual or short-lived perennial. 2 centimetres to 5 centimetres. Zone 5.

Stonecrop (*Sedum acre*) has tiny, moss-like, light green leaves and yellow flowers in summer. It's best planted on the outer edges of your path, as sedum is easily crushed. 5 centimetres. Zone 2.

Creeping mazus (*Mazus reptans*) creates a fast-spreading, bright green mat that accepts some foot traffic. Lavender flowers cover the plant in spring, and even if dieback occurs during winter, it will come back. Can be aggressive. Sun or part shade. 5 centimetres. Zone 4.

Woolly thyme (*Thymus pseudolanuginosus*) has a fuzzy texture and grey-green colour; when stepped on, its leaves release their distinctive fragrance. Small, pink flowers appear in early summer. Low-growing thymes accept fairly heavy foot traffic and actually prefer nutrient-poor soil. Able to thrive in dry conditions. Sun or part shade. 2.5 centimetres. Zone 2. ∎

Water, rocks and a hint of Japanese design help create quiet city retreats

serenity gardens

174 SERENE AND STYLISH

182 DREAM RETREAT

188 CONTEMPLATING
    PARADISE

196 ORIENTAL VARIATIONS

204 URBAN OASIS

GARDEN PROJECT
210 CREATING A POND
216 PLANTS FOR PONDS

serene
andstylish

VANCOUVER SEEMS A WORLD AWAY IN THIS JAPANESE-STYLE GARDEN
BY SHIRLEY BLEVINS

East meets West in Bill Walters' well-tended garden, styled after Japan's Momoyama period, when colour was popular. The garden was designed to look good even on Vancouver's greyest days, with plenty of form and texture in plants, rocks and artifacts to enhance the beautiful blooms Bill loves.

In the heart of Vancouver's Shaughnessy neighbourhood, mere feet away from a traffic-filled street, lies an unexpectedly pastoral scene. It's Bill Walter's Japanese-style garden, filled with the clean fragrance of pine and a mosaic of textures, forms and colours, as well as the gentle sound of water cascading into a koi-filled pond. Even at rush hour, the garden offers a tranquil sanctuary from the outside world.

Like millions of Canadians, Bill turns to his garden for rejuvenation. "I enjoy working in it," he says. "It gives me a chance to express my creativity." And when he isn't working in it, he's contemplating it. "It's a four-season garden, attractive at many times of the year."

In early spring, marsh marigolds, daffodils and primula predominate; in April and May, the rhododendrons, azaleas and wisteria flourish, followed by a proliferation of irises and hostas. Next come the perennials, succeeded in late summer by asters and lilies, and blue pickerel weed (*Pontederia cordata*) in the bog garden. In fall, the red foliage of the maples, the golden leaves of the birches and the red, pink and white blooms of the kaffir lily (*Schizostylis coccinea*) add accents of colour. A palette of greens, punctuated with viburnum, flowering jasmine and hellebore, thrives throughout winter, and after a fresh snowfall (which happens occasionally in Vancouver), the garden is "awesome,"

Guests occasionally catch dinner in the trout run at the bottom of the garden, which rises in a sculpted hill to the back. The bamboo railing deters heron from fishing. Every window across the back of the house has a view of the garden. Below right: flat stones set in Corsican mint lead to a bench on the upper level.

according to Bill. "Even on the dullest, wettest days, it's still beautiful."

The garden was, in fact, designed to work well on those grey, overcast Vancouver days. Sculpted evergreens set against a mosaic of granite rocks and interspersed with Japanese statuary, such as metal cranes, metal and stone lanterns, and stone temple statues, look their best in subdued light. But, as Bill points out, his garden is as much about style as it is about content.

In the Japanese tradition, the garden focuses more on form and texture—the vertical bamboo, the spreading maples, the spiky pines, the feathery cypress—than on colour. "Japanese gardens depict nature in a semi-stylized fashion, with an eye toward proportion and the balance of shapes, textures and other elements," he says. A few noteworthy elements in his garden include the deer scarer and *kakeki* stick (water spout). But Bill isn't a purist—he can't ignore his love of flowers and jokingly describes his garden as "Japenglish"—Japanese style, but with lots of perennials.

In fact, Brian Clarke, the landscape designer and contractor who designed and built Bill's garden in 1988, styled it after the Momoyama period of Japanese garden history, when colour was popular.

Ironically, Bill's Japanese-style garden germinated from water: the original garden was plagued with serious drainage problems and in need of renovation. When Bill and his family moved into the house in 1978, the back garden consisted of a lawn that sloped steeply down toward the house from the street behind, with rhododendrons, pines, maples and lots of pernicious weeds. Bill eventually got rid of the weeds, thinned out the vegetation and developed a small Japanese garden, but the drainage tiles at the bottom of the slope regularly filled up with mud and had to be dug up, cleaned out and re-set. That's when Bill called in Brian, who specializes in water gardens.

The design concept started with a dry streambed that would flow down the sides of the property. "Then we decided, well, let's do a bit of a pond," Bill says. "And what about a waterfall?" The project mushroomed into a major facelift that began with a BobCat sculpting the sloping property, splitting it into levels, carving out an alcove and creating a pathway from bottom to top. The next step was the installation of the various underground systems—plumbing, sprinkler, electrical and, most important, drainage.

To analyze the drainage problem, Brian needed to know the subterranean secrets of the property. He found the original survey, which showed the neighbourhood had once contained a lake drained by about 60 creeks and an untold number of springs. The CPR, which started developing the area around the turn of the century, filled in the lake and creeks with everything from boulders to parts of wrecked trains. "We actually found locomotive boiler tubing when excavating the backyard," Brian says.

They also discovered a belt of pristine Surrey blue clay, three separate layers of fossilized seashells, a boulder-filled creek and six springs, all still running. "We had to deal with fine particles of clay that clogged the drain tiles, plus an immense

low-key lighting

The Walters can enjoy their garden from dusk to dawn if they wish, thanks to a variety of decorative lights. Marine lights mounted on posts light the stairs, and Japanese-style box lanterns made from metal and sheets of opaque plastic focus on the grass pathway and highlight parts of the garden. A couple of antique Japanese bronze lanterns illuminate the teahouse, and two attractive stone lanterns double as garden art and garden lights. There's also a wooden lantern resembling a miniature wooden house with windows on each side (seen at left), which both decorates and illuminates.

The Japanese box lanterns are replicas of a light that garden designer Brian Clarke retrieved from a demolished 1930s apartment building. The two stone lanterns, which he designed and fabricated, are made of wooden boxes covered with large, flat rocks on which moss and succulents grow (see opening page).

The garden lighting is subdued (bulbs no stronger than 15 watts are used) to provide soft, gentle illumination in keeping with the tone of the garden.

amount of water that made the soil wet, sour and fetid," Brian says. To solve the problem, he designed an enormous drainage system. "We riddled the place with big drainage intercepts." In addition, the drainage tiles were bagged in geotextile (filter cloth) to prevent the fine blue clay from plugging them. The result: good drainage and more friable soil that allowed for a lush, healthy garden.

At the lowest part of the garden nearest the house, an excavation was made to create a trout run, which functions as a collecting reservoir for the waterfall. By this time, 40 truckloads of soil had been removed from the property.

Next came the rocks. "I had no idea the size of the rocks that would be coming in," Bill says. More than 90 metric tonnes of rock, ranging from 2 kilograms to 18.5 metric tonnes each, were distributed throughout the garden and installed to make the pond and stream. This part of the garden took one full season to

The teahouse, on an upper level at one side of the garden, is both guesthouse and mini-retreat, where Bill putters in the workshop or practises his cello. It's reached via a curving stone path, seen below right. In front of the teahouse is a cypress pruned to look as if clouds are perching at the end of its branches.

design and build and, as Bill puts it, "It cost a few bucks." It's been growing and developing ever since.

The teahouse was started in 1991 and gestated in a similar fashion to the garden. "I thought it would be nice to have a small gazebo and a hot tub," Bill says.

"Then the gazebo idea started to grow." The resulting 90-square-metre teahouse contains a gym, workshop and a traditional Japanese guest room with tatami mats, a sunken tub and Japanese antiques. Bill spends many of his evenings in the teahouse, exercising in

the gym, puttering in the workshop or practising his cello—that is, when he's not working in the garden, which keeps him and his gardener, Michael Latimer, busy year-round. "We spend most of our time trying to keep everything in scale," Bill says. "This means a lot of pruning.

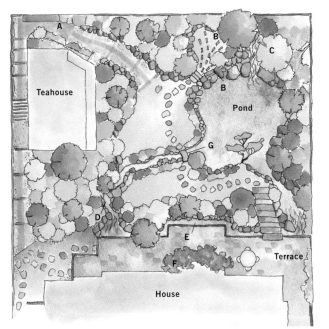

Teahouse

Pond

G

D

E

F

Terrace

House

A Japanese gate
B Bench
C Upper waterfall
D Lower waterfall
E Trout run
F Wisteria
G Bridge

(30 x 18 metres)

If I let plants go, I'd be in big trouble because the garden is intensely planted."

Bill uses 490-centimetre tripod tree ladders to reach the trees. He does most of the pruning, a key element in Japanese gardens. He's learned about Japanese-style pruning through working with Brian Clarke, reading books on the subject and looking at a lot of photos and drawings. "I sort of have a feel for what was done traditionally," he says.

Michael shares some of the pruning chores as well as Bill's passion for the garden. He spends at least an hour a day there, even in winter. "I keep the waterfalls running, back-flush the filters, weed, spread the compost, clear out old growth

and carry out Bill's ideas," he says.

Bill's garden is home to more than trout and koi. Turtles and crayfish share the fish habitat, and a healthy frog population keeps the bugs in check and serenades the Walters at night. "But the ones that croak get eaten by the raccoons," says Bill, who enjoys watching these backyard bandits, even if they do nab the occasional trout.

Bill's favourite wildlife visitors are the mallard ducks that come almost daily to swim in the pond and gobble up proffered corn snacks. One particular pair has been coming for nearly 10 years and considers the place theirs. "They're not afraid of us," says Bill. "If they come and there's no food, they walk down to the patio and tap on the door." And they chase away all other mallard intruders. "If other ducks come to visit, all hell breaks loose," he laughs. "A whole lot of quackin' and flappin' goes on."

Bill is never far from the garden—the kitchen, dining room, living room and bedrooms of the glass-and-concrete home all look out on the garden. In fact, strategic views of the waterfalls from key areas in the house are no accident. "The garden is a passion of Bill's," Michael says. "He can relax in it, or he can get very excited about it when he's thinking of new things to try."

backyardfishing

Many gardens have koi ponds, but few boast a trout run filled with a hundred or more rainbow trout. Bill Walter's deep trout run (24 metres long by 60 to 150 centimetres wide and 90 centimetres deep) resembles a woodland stream bordered with rocks and plants. There's no sign of the sunken pressure-treated plywood box and steel-rib supports that form the streambed.

The stream flows along the low side of the sloping yard bordering the edge of the patio. At one end is a 180- by 180-centimetre spawning bed, 15 centimetres deep. Although the trout go through the motions of spawning, Bill says they have yet to produce hatchlings. Usually, about one hundred trout thrive in the run, some weighing as much as 3.6 kilograms.

Rather than scooping them out of the run with a net when trout is on the menu, the family and sometimes the guests try their luck at fishing. "It's fun for the kids," says Bill. The preferred bait is worms, but the trout occasionally strike at flies. The largest of the fish, the survivors, are treated more like pets than groceries, and if caught are released. The trout were also dinner for visiting herons until Bill and designer Brian Clarke constructed a 20-centimetre-high bamboo railing to discourage the long-legged poachers. The space is already confined and the railing further restricts it, preventing the birds from crouching down—a manoeuvre necessary for catching fish.

pruningJapanese-style

"The heart and soul of Japanese pruning—and there are many different styles of pruning—is simplify, simplify, simplify," says landscape designer Brian Clarke. "Remove branches and create more character in the branches you've got."

Brian recommends gardeners keep in mind the general direction they want the plant to grow and remember that the primary source of light the plant receives affects this direction.

For example, because Bill's garden grows on a north-facing slope and has lots of trees, only a few corners receive sunlight year-round. And because trees naturally grow toward light, Bill says he can forget trying to train them in another direction.

Pruning Japanese-style is labour-intensive. In order to control the growth of his pine trees, Bill breaks off about three-quarters of the length of all but a few candles (the new growth in spring). This forces the growth of many smaller candles that would otherwise remain dormant; these may be subsequently thinned out. If candles are kept small, they don't grow into branches. In addition, Bill removes all but this year's and last year's needles from the inner branches.

"Japanese gardeners also prune branches to make them look like clouds," Bill says, pointing to a cypress tree near the teahouse (see previous spread). To achieve "clouds" of foliage, he trims back all the inside growth (foliage and small branches) and leaves a puff of foliage at the end of each large branch.

Bill uses similar techniques on other trees and shrubs, such as the junipers by the pond and in the facing photo. If he's trying for a bonsai look, he may prune back some of the main branches. On the branches he retains, he prunes the inner part, leaving balls of foliage at the tips. "But if you really want to be fancy," Bill says, "you prune up underneath so the remaining tiny branches become exposed like little fingers, and you just leave a bit of foliage on the top. You can choose whatever shape you want," he adds. "But in this case, you end up with long, bare branches terminating in a bunch of fingers at the tip supporting a platter of foliage." Cutting back some of the foliage exposes the shape of the trunk and branches and allows more light to pass through; it also offers less obstructed views of the garden.

"I know some experts are shocked at what I do to my maples," Bill shrugs, "but I've got to keep things in scale; otherwise, the plants underneath don't get sufficient light. When I prune every other year, I take so much out of these trees, I think I'm not going to have any branches left, but they always come back." ▪

dreamretreat

A REGINA COUPLE DESIGN A SIMPLE AND HARMONIOUS GARDEN
BY MARGARET HRYNIUK

A new house with a small yard in a suburban development offered a Regina couple the chance to create what they'd always wanted: a low-maintenance Japanese-style garden. A family project, it took four years of teamwork and follows many principles of Japanese design—simplicity, balance, restraint and repetition.

When Joanne and Dave Mumford's son, Dylan, moved away from home, the Regina couple faced their empty nest by moving to a new nest—and creating the serene Japanese garden that had long been their dream. For years, the Mumfords had been attracted to the stillness and harmony of Japanese gardens, seeking them out during their travels. They hadn't really considered making a Japanese-style garden, however, because the main feature of their former home was a swimming pool, which dictated the landscaping.

Their new home, built in 1994 in a suburban development, had a small, 14-metre-square backyard that lent itself perfectly to the Japanese style. It also let them plan for a low-maintenance garden—"where we could eventually relax," Joanne says.

The new garden was four years in the making. First, they read books on the principles of a Japanese garden. Recognition and enhancement of each season's beauty is an important element; *mie gakure*, a Japanese phrase meaning "hide and reveal" or "pause and see different views," is another. Balance, which creates harmony, is partly achieved with natural materials that emphasize both vertical and horizontal elements. Simplicity is key.

Following these principles in Regina's heavy clay, known as gumbo, and the extremes of

A low wooden bridge, left, crosses the dry streambed and links two patios, one embedded with an off-centre pond; golden-rod, grasses and creeping junipers grow along the creekbed. The dramatic zigzag wooden path, seen in the background and on the previous page, changes levels five times and is anchored with cedar posts to suggest a dock over water.

its Zone 2b climate, kept Joanne at her gardening books and graph paper for the first two winters. Implementing her design kept Dave fit for most of the summers as he moved river rocks and large boulders, and built the deck, two arbours, walkways, a fence and two patios.

"A lot of the design ideas are mine, but Dave is the backbone of this garden," Joanne admits. Or, as Dave says, "Joanne gets an idea and I get a backache."

For example, the back door opened onto a drop of just over a metre, so Joanne thought a raised deck would serve as a transition from the house to the privacy of the ground-level garden. Dave built a narrow deck with wide steps on risers that couldn't be seen: "I wanted each step to appear to be floating," Joanne says. He also carted out the gumbo, wheeled in the topsoil and peat moss and, with Dylan's help, hauled in several boulders hand-picked by Joanne from farmers' fields.

Together, Dave and Dylan created two patios of 45-centimetre concrete pavers, each separated from the other by exactly 2 centimetres of pea gravel. Both patios are the same size—3.6 metres square—but one is near the foot of the steps to the deck, the other toward the back of the yard.

The small stones at a side entrance and the river rock in a dry creek echo the pea gravel of the patios. The dry creek

meanders from the west corner of the house, under the gently curved bridge, to the opposite corner of the garden. "In a Japanese garden, repeating elements is one way to achieve balance," Joanne says. "But balance and harmony do not necessarily mean symmetry."

Dave built four chairs and a low, round table for one patio, and two chairs and a side table for the other. He also built the bridge over the dry creek—a low, wide arch of cedar planks that harmonizes with two identical cedar arbours placed at right angles at opposite sides of the yard. Each frames a vignette of stone and greenery that can be viewed from the sitting area on the first patio.

During the second, third and fourth years of the garden's evolution, Joanne and Dave placed plants chosen for subtle colour and texture and their contribution to the seasons. To contrast with snow, they planted evergreens, including dwarf mugo and Scotch pines. Balancing the different varieties of horizontal junipers are two Tolleson's weeping junipers (*Juniperus scopulorum* 'Tolleson's Weeping'), which Joanne read about in one of Lois Hole's books. She reasoned that if they were hardy enough for Edmonton, they'd be hardy enough in her

protected Regina garden. And they are.

The challenging climate meant that Joanne and Dave had to substitute hardier plants for those found in a Japanese garden. Flowering crabapple trees— 'Thunderchild', 'Radiant' and weeping 'Red Jade'—are more robust than the cherry trees of Japan, yet evoke a similar feeling. Joanne takes particular pleasure in the winter-hardy bluebird clematis (*Clematis macropetala* 'Blue Bird') that blooms on the arbours and a fence in spring and again in late summer.

The plants get no extra protection in winter. "The snow brings them through," Joanne says, pointing out the sturdy daylilies, ferns, hostas, Siberian irises and two dwarf golden elders: 'Golden Plume' and 'Golden Locks'. The elders and the creamy-yellow blooms of the

Plants were chosen for texture, subtle colour and seasonal interest. A variety of heights is emphasized, and yellow flowers such as goldenrod and daylilies echo through the garden. Below left: a basin and three stones, part of the tea ceremony. The basin is for water, the right stone for the ladle, the left holds the visitor's belongings, and the centre stone is to stand on.

'Stella d'Oro' daylily provide the only colour in the green palette of high summer. In autumn, the golden elders contrast with the gorgeous red of an amur maple (*Acer ginnala*), an ornamental tree chosen for its similarity to a Japanese maple, as well as for its hardiness.

The garden evolved, but not in a haphazard way. After much research and discussion, Joanne and Dave decided to replace the small, seldom-used lawn beyond the patios with a zigzagging wooden path surrounded by plants.

"Zigzagging bridges encourage you to take many turns and forget the constraints of time and space," says Joanne. "The Yatsuhashi—meaning eight bridges—with irises alongside them date back to ancient Japanese literary figures who admired the irises growing along the eight channels of the Azuma River, each with its own bridge. It is also thought that on crooked bridges one can avoid evil spirits, which flow in straight lines."

Once again, there was compromise.

Dave built a modified zigzag composed of eight sections of cedar planks. The levels of the sections change five times to prompt the feeling of movement through a much larger space. Each section is anchored with cedar posts to suggest a dock suspended over water.

Water is essential in a Japanese garden. In a square pond in the back patio, fish glide through rushes, waterlilies, dwarf bamboo and water hyacinths. The second water feature, a grey granite birdbath, is set in a bed of small, black river rocks like those in the dry creek. Beside it is a granite snow lantern, so named because snow is caught in interesting shapes on its roof.

Because odd numbers are most pleasing in a garden, Joanne and Dave set a third water vignette in a square of pebbles representing the sea. It contains a Zenigata, a type of basin used in tea ceremonies, and three stones. Traditionally, participants placed anything they were carrying on the stone on the left; the stone on the right held the ladle used to scoop up water from the basin to rinse the hands. The front stone was for standing on.

Softening the edges of every vignette is woolly thyme. This use of one kind of ground cover illustrates another basic of Japanese gardens: restraint. It does not come easily to Joanne. "I haven't met a plant I didn't like, but the repetitive use of plant materials is more restful to the eye," she admits.

"Joanne is very creative," Dave says. Joanne replies: "And you've learned how to build." Their harmonious teamwork has resulted in a garden that more than fulfills their long-cherished dream. ▪

contemplating paradise

PEACE AND SERENITY PREVAIL IN A CALGARY ROCK GARDEN
BY SUZANNE ZWARUN

William Schrader felt a mystical connection to the Rockies as soon as he saw them, and he's filled his garden with rocks that speak to him as the mountains do. But the garden also contains a tapestry of plants carefully selected to mimic nature and to create an atmosphere of peace and harmony.

William Schrader has always marched to the beat of a different drummer. When family and friends were reconstructing their lives after the Second World War, the 21-year-old fled Germany for a new life in a land he perceived as a peaceful paradise. Eventually, he settled in Calgary, and when he started gardening there, in 1958, he planted a conventional lawn bordered by flowers.

But that didn't last long. William Schrader, like Thoreau, needed the tonic of wilderness. So he has perched, piled and tumbled rocks throughout his garden, recreating the rugged grandeur of the mountains in his southwest Calgary neighbourhood. "What kind of garden is this?" he asks, repeating a question he is often asked. "You tell me."

A tangled English country garden it's not. William felt a mystical connection to the Rocky Mountains from the moment he saw them, and he's combined the brutal beauty of their rocks with the subtle tranquillity of a Japanese garden to create a harmonious whole that's not easily defined. It's a rockery, but it lacks the exotic alpine plants you'd expect to find in one. It's a perennial garden, but the number of species is sharply limited, and ordinary plants have often been sculpted into extraordinary tapestries with the exquisite detail of petit point needlework. It's a garden focused on trees, but many arrived accidentally—"gifts of the birds"—and all

of them baffle and delight visitors because they've been pruned as dramatically as bonsai.

What kind of garden is this? It's a garden that invites contemplation. "This garden plays with all your senses—sound, sight, smell," William says. "And your thoughts dwell on deeper things."

The mountains beckoned William to Calgary from Ontario, where he had first settled and met his German-born wife, Ingrid. "I dreamed about the Rockies, and told her such stories that she said she'd give it a try." They left for Calgary the day after they were married, in 1955. Within a week of their arrival, William found work with the city, and they bought their house three years later. His fellow workers considered the house a mere starter. Not William: "I wanted a home to last me a lifetime. I wanted roots."

He immediately set to planting some, although Calgarians warned him that gardening in the Chinook belt was a waste of time and money. "I couldn't accept that. I come from a lush country. I cannot live on the open prairie. I cannot live with just one tree."

In those days his lot was big and bare, on the southern edge of the city next to

farmland. The house sits at the base of a steeply angled triangle that's 21 metres on the south side, which adjoins the back lane, and 60 metres on the west side. Schrader had a friend with a farm tractor rearrange the earth, creating slopes out of flat land and making a 2.4-metre-high mini-mountain at the apex of the triangle.

Then he dug up one hundred seedlings, each about 8 centimetres tall, from the Persian lilac hedge (*Syringa persica*) that grew on the property he and Ingrid had been renting. He planted them along

both sides of the new property. Now, they totally encircle the backyard, forming a 3-metre-tall barrier that's impenetrable to wind and the whine of traffic on a nearby busy thoroughfare. "The secret to this yard is that it's completely sheltered," William says. "Anything that grows below the hedge grows well."

So did two 40-year-old laurel-leaf willows (*Salix pentandra*), although they now tower over the hedge. One crowns the mini-mountain he calls his meditation area; the other embraces the patio like a living umbrella. William used a trick he remembered from Germany to start the

House plants summer outdoors in and around the pond William built beside the house so the music of the waterfall can be heard. Opposite page: the view from his dining room, through large windows installed to appreciate it. Lily-of-the-valley and primulas wend their way through the front rockery.

willows: he pruned a friend's willows, selecting branches about 15 centimetres in diameter. He cut them 180 centimetres long and buried them upright 60 centimetres deep, packing the earth tightly. Roots developed at the nodes where there had been smaller branches; above ground, other nodes produced new branches that he shaped as they grew.

Some trees he tried in the beginning— cedars, ornamentals from eastern mail-order catalogues—didn't do so well. The Schraders, who raised a son and a dozen foster children over the years, spent every weekend camping in the mountains when the children were growing up. "When I saw that things grew there, I thought, why not try local stuff?" He started harvesting junipers and spruce from roadside utility areas, plants destined to die from regular applications of herbicides. "It hurts me to see something die," he says.

He rescued rocks, too, retrieving them from the sites of new subdivisions, or inheriting them from friends who abandoned planned rock gardens when they discovered the work involved. "The rocks all have special meaning, related to what was here before," says William, who sought out sandstone formed by the retreat of the sea that covered southern Alberta, and granite deposited by glaci-

ers. "You can get stories out of rocks if you can connect with them," he says, pointing out a bluish rock from Banff embedded with shell fossils 400 million years old; it's close to another one with 50-thousand-year-old fossils. In one restful spot, he's arranged greyish-white stones from an Italian beach in a graceful shallow bowl, a replica of one from ancient Rome. "This is an imitation of ancient times, with real pebbles that lay for tens of thousands of years on a beach," he says, his imagination fired by the juxtaposition of the two. "Rocks aren't alive, but they're so powerful they make you feel humble."

His vision of how to use rocks in his garden came straight from the mountains he loves so passionately. "Nothing in this yard is abruptly cut off, the way we do with our buildings," he says. "Rocks fall in the mountains in different layers, in different directions. And in between the rocks, plants come up. No earth shows."

William deliberately limits the varieties of plants in his garden. "Nature has a system," he says. "Mountain meadows are beautiful flower gardens that took

thousands of years to develop. But I found no more than six species in any one place, due to the conditions of the soil there. Having hundreds of species of flowers together is a greenhouse concept that doesn't exist in nature."

At first, William tried moving mountain species to his garden, but because the soil conditions were different, they lived only a few years. He opted instead for cultivated species that mimic mountain plants. A sprawl of sedums under spruce trees mirrors the common stonecrop (*Sedum steno-petalum*) that grows wild in cracks and crevices in rocky places. Two clumps of cyclamen blossoming at the base of a spruce tree look like wild shooting star, and belong to the same family. Wild roses flank a Grootendorst rose that's new enough to still have its nursery tag. (Little else in the garden bears a tag, so William knows everything from iris to columbine by their common names. "I'm not a

botanist or a Latinist. At my age, their names are not important any more.")

William allows flowers a vital, albeit limited, role in his garden. "You have to have a few bright spots. With rocks you slow down. Flowers give you the high pitches." A yellow stream of leopard's bane (*Doronicum* spp.), blankets of lily-of-the-valley, tulips and primulas hit high notes in spring. But much of the beauty of the garden depends on foliage, like the colourful quilt stitched by a mass of red, orange and green hens-and-chickens in a sunny bed on the west side of the house.

The emphasis on shapes and the ever-changing play of light on plants gives the garden life year-round. William long ago installed floor-to-ceiling windows in the house to allow him the virtual reality of being outside when he's indoors. "This garden is never dead. Flowers are here for the shortest period, but with the rocks visible under the snow, with the textures of plants, the way I trimmed the trees, it's a garden 12 months of the year."

It's not a garden needing constant care, however. William says he seldom sees a weed. Dandelions plague his neighbours, but they don't penetrate his garden. His policy of leaving no earth exposed discourages weeds from rooting, except for errant Manitoba maple seedlings, which seem to sprout in concrete. His garden wasn't always maintenance-free—he remembers years of backbreaking labour, lifting stones again and again to root out plants and weeds running rampant.

"A rockery is a lot more work than grass and annuals. The first five years was hard work. Weeding between rocks is no fun." Now, his chores are shaping trees and maintaining the meticulously manicured lilac hedge he prunes by hand—a two-day job—so as not to tear the oversize leaves that are up to 13 centimetres long.

For William, shaping trees is a labour of love, not work. That's lucky, because it takes a great deal of work to coax normally untidy trees like the laurel-leaf willow into spare, dramatic shapes. "Every tree shoots straight toward the sun, but in the mountains the winds push them," he says. "Here, I push every tree in a certain direction. It's very selfish of me, but I rescue them and I demand something of them."

He demanded that a mountain ash (*Sorbus americana*) fit under a spruce tree and trained it to branch like a hand with fingers outspread beseechingly. His demands on a clump of black birch (*Betula occidentalis*) produced a tangle of trunks Medusa would envy. And even though the willows are 15 metres high now, he's still sculpting them, working on the "spokes" of his umbrellas, shortening branches to straighten them and keep them from breaking under the weight of snow.

He shaped a peach tree that rooted itself from a dropped pit a decade ago into a true bonsai—it grows horizontally, a mere 45 centimetres tall, beside the front steps. William has, in fact, adapted bonsai techniques to miniaturize many of his trees. "Bonsai involves cutting the roots as well as the tops," he says. In his garden, the roots of the willows and the lilacs similarly check the growth of other roots. He fertilizes nothing, not even adding manure to soil so depleted he says it won't support annuals. And yet plants thrive. He attributes this to a native spirituality similar to shamanism, which theorizes that energy fields fuel each other. "The energy of this area, generated by the sun and the rocks, lets certain things grow here," he says. "The energy field harmonizes everything."

The reaction of visitors to his garden fascinates him. People who arrive chattering and laughing emerge silent, visibly moved by the garden. People ask to stay longer, to return another time. Again and again, they tell him they feel they've stepped into paradise.

His story has come full circle, William says. The young man who arrived in Canada seeking paradise found it by creating a haven. "My spirituality is in nature. I don't expect people to feel the same way but, seeing them here, I realize it's their spirituality as well. People need this. When I realized that, I got my reward for sharing."

A dry streambed accented with rocks and upright logs runs along the pathway leading to the back garden; in wet weather it drains away excess water from a downspout. Trees are carefully pruned to bring out their innate beauty and character and let in sunshine. The rocks and the sun in his garden generate the energy to make things grow, William says.

designingwithrocks

There are well-made rock gardens, but there are more instances, particularly in public places, where boulders have been plunked down as if gargantuan gods had suddenly abandoned a game of lawn bowls. William Schrader is more creative, taking his cue from the mountains he loves. "My teachers were the Rockies, the foothills," he says.

He's turned his front yard into the kind of gentle, rocky slope you'd find in the foothills, carpeting it with the 4.5-metre sprawl of an ancient, native juniper, whose twisted branches look like modern art. The mini-mountain in the farthest corner of his backyard was inspired by higher terrain and requires a serious climb up the flat layers, which serve as steps to the summit.

At one corner of the house, angular blocks and slices of shale are so reminiscent of a scree slope that you almost expect the small mountain mammal called a pica to pop up. In fact, a downspout has been fed into the rubble, so when it rains, torrents of water cascade down the rocks and into an otherwise dry streambed, its bottom spread with mosses and lichen. Then it drains into the ever-thirsty Persian lilacs (*Syringa persica*). During dry spells, William turns on a hose, also hidden in the scree slope.

A self-taught mason, William spent years building walls inside the house and alongside the patio, developing a technique of washing away the visible mortar so the rocks seem to be stacked in natural strata rather than in a manmade pattern. He can also employ a single stone effectively. Walk through the garden gate in late afternoon and see how the sun pierces a piece of petrified sequoia thrust upright against a green background. The rock stands like a sentinel, spotlighted by a shaft of the Western sun, a bolt of light from the heavens. □

oriental variations

A SUCCESSFUL ZEN GARDEN THAT DOESN'T FOLLOW ALL THE RULES
BY PAUL MARSHMAN

Real Japanese gardens follow set rules, but not Joseph and Paulie Marmina's. Still, they worked hard to achieve the aesthetics and contemplative spirit of the Oriental style, using accessories like the Buddha and lantern in the side garden, right. The lattice and pruned tree also have a Japanese flavour. Left: stones and sempervivum in pots

For Joseph and Paulie Marmina, nothing is more relaxing than a serene Oriental landscape, especially the one that's as close as their front door. From the Japanese sitting deck of their Toronto home they can look out on a still life they created themselves.

Joseph and Paulie call it their tranquillity garden. It took its present form five years ago, when they decided to create a Japanese-style garden at the front of the house to complement the ones in a similar style

alongside and behind it. A visitor entering through the traditional raffia-bound bamboo gate—hand-built by the Marminas—can't help but be struck by the instant contrast with the busy street just outside.

A broad flagstone pathway takes you through an astonishingly varied miniature landscape: a dry riverbed surrounded by blue-hued evergreens, Japanese maple, blue spruce, yew and mulberry, and ornamental grasses benignly guarded by a smiling Buddha. As it nears the house, the pathway narrows so you can stop and admire a small "mountain" planted with bonsai trees and sedums. A trickle of water flows down from its peak into a small pond where goldfish feed among waterlilies, water hyacinths, and a variety of other plants, including tropical taro and papyrus. A thicket of hostas, mosses and ferns grows around the pool.

Stone for the garden was chosen and placed with great care—smooth, flat stones for the dry streambed so they look worn by water; rough boulders set deep in soil or plantings so they look natural. Driftwood and pieces of old tree limbs are also incorporated into the landscape, which looks like a miniature vista of blending colours and textures.

accused me of doing it secretly," Paulie laughs, "but I told him wild crocuses grow in the mountains of Japan, so they should stay."

The stones are chosen and placed with care. "In the streams, we have tried to pick smooth, flat stones that represent water flowing over them," Paulie says, adding that the colour of the stones is tested wet as well as dry to make sure the garden looks attractive even in wet weather. "Joel even waters the rocks sometimes for special occasions—they look sensational wet."

Most of the plants come from commercial nurseries, but sometimes the Marminas have saved money by buying "no-name" unlabelled plants and damaged or misshapen shrubs that were going to be tossed out—just right for a garden of interesting shapes. As their confidence grows, however, Paulie says they're beginning to move toward more expensive, choice varieties such as Japanese peonies.

The garden is low maintenance—beds are mulched using homemade leaf compost and pine needles to retain moisture and discourage weeds, and landscape fabric under the flagstone paths prevents weeds from growing through. An especially heavy layer of pine needles and evergreen branches is applied over many of the plants in winter and removed in spring. Manure and compost are added each year to improve the soil.

Joseph likes to use bamboo poles to enhance the shape of shrubs and trees, positioning them so that they support branches or pull them down or back.

Pruning the trees and shrubs to maintain the scale of the garden is the most critical upkeep. "That's my hobby," he says.

"We work five days a week, and the other two days we're in the garden," Joseph says. But when the work is done and it's time to enjoy their labours, he and Paulie like to sit on a couple of rocks by the dry riverbed with a glass of wine and take pleasure in the quiet.

"We didn't want the garden to be just decorative," Paulie says. "We wanted to use it as a place to do things: sit, read, listen to the water, watch the birds, talk. It truly is a sanctuary."

splendid grasses

Ornamental grasses add height and colour to any garden, helping fill in sparse areas and, in winter, offering contrasting notes of beige and gold against the snow with their dry stems.

The Marminas' garden includes more than a dozen ornamental grasses, ranging from blue oats (*Helictotrichon sempervirens*) and fountain grass (*Pennisetum alopecuroides*) to Japanese bloodgrass (*Imperata cylindrica* 'Red Baron') and six types of maiden grass: *Miscanthus sinensis*, 'Gracillimus', 'Morning Light', *M. purpurascens*, 'Zebrinus' and 'Nippon'.

Here are some key things to consider before buying and planting ornamental grasses and a few suggestions from Paulie Marmina.

WINTER HARDINESS

Some temperate-zone species, such as blue oat-grass, are hardy to Zone 4, while most bamboos thrive best in Zones 7 and 8, restricting them to the British Columbia coast.

SIZE

Some grasses, such as northern sea oats, are 1 metre to 1.5 metres at full height. Others, such as the aptly named *Miscanthus sinensis giganteus*, grow to 4 metres and dominate the garden. Plant a large grass by itself, leaving enough space for it to reach its potential.

SHAPE

Ornamental grasses grow in a variety of shapes: mound forming, open spreading, upright arching, upright narrow, and upright open. Find a picture of the plant at maturity to see if it's suitable for the site you have in mind.

REQUIREMENTS

Grasses are suited to different conditions, depending on their native habitats. Most require well-drained sites in full sun, but some tolerate moist soil and shade; others prefer boggy sites or ponds. Variegated grasses, for example, blister in strong sunlight. For full shade, consider *Carex elata* 'Bowles Golden', *C. nigra* or *Deschampsia*; in wet sites, *Glyceria*, *Deschampsia* or *Miscanthus sinensis* are good choices.

COMBINATIONS

Grasses are best with plants that have contrasting texture and colour. Fountain grasses look wonderful in front of a green background such as a stand of evergreens, while others, such as *Miscanthus sinensis*, Japanese bloodgrass and *Hakonechioa*, look best when the sunlight shines through them. Reference books can suggest successful companions.

PLANTING

In the right spot, ornamental grasses will thrive (and often multiply) for years without special care. Before you buy, check a good reference book—the information provided by nurseries can be sketchy. Beware of invasive grasses, which include many of the rhizomatous and stoloniferous species. Nurseries should warn you before you buy, but the friend who offers you a clump for free may not. Notorious spreaders are lyme grasses and species of *Phalaris.* Plant perennial grasses in the spring, digging a hole one and a half times the size of the root ball. Surround the roots with a mixture of equal parts peat moss, manure or other humus, and sand. Add super-phosphate fertilizer (0–20–0) to the backfill, using 30 mL per bushel. Allow spacing between plants equal to the height of the plant at maturity, although this may be impossible with some larger grasses.

MAINTENANCE

Grasses can be left through the winter, but should be cut down to about 5 centimetres in early spring so the old material won't spoil the look of the new year's growth.

urbanoasis

THE MIRACLE OF MAKING A GARDEN SANCTUARY IN A COLD CLIMATE
BY STEPHANIE WHITTAKER

A popular song and a neighbour helped persuade Cinea and Habib Daoud that gardening in Montreal was worthwhile, and within a few short years their austere yard was transformed into a private sanctuary. It's especially beautiful in fall, when berries, red and gold leaves and grasses cascade over weathered decking and aging pavers.

For more than 20 years after she had immigrated to Montreal, Cinea de Souza Daoud resisted the idea of planting a garden. A native of Brazil, Cinea saw no reason to cultivate plants outdoors in a country that's "covered in snow for a third of the year." Her husband, Habib, who had emigrated from Syria and met Cinea at the Royal Victoria Hospital, where they both worked as doctors, did not share her reservations. He'd started a vegetable patch behind their charming 1913 home in the Outremont area of Montreal, which they bought in 1980. But it wasn't enough; he yearned for an ornamental garden, reminiscent of those he'd known in the Middle East.

It was the lyrics of "Mon Pays," a well-known song by the Quebec poet-singer Gilles Vigneault, that finally persuaded Cinea that gardening in a cold climate had its rewards. The song extols the virtues of winter with these opening lines: "*Mon pays, ce n'est pas un pays, c'est l'hiver. Mon jardin, ce n'est pas un jardin, c'est la neige.*" [My country is not a country, it's winter. My garden is not a garden, it's snow.]

Then, there was the fact that the Daouds had had their kitchen renovated so that it opened into an adjacent solarium, giving them a new view of their backyard, which had previously been easy to ignore. "The view was ugly. There was no garden when

The fourth zone is a dining area that's well used by family and friends throughout the gardening season and borders on the pond. "In the morning, I have *café au lait* here," says Cinea. "In the evenings, we have barbecues. We eat outside almost every evening right into the autumn. We're often joined by visitors from Brazil or by my husband's family from Syria." There are also visits from their daughter, Maya, and their son, Alexandre.

Plenty of features around the outdoor dining area provide a feast for the eyes: ornamental grasses and hydrangeas offer botanical interest, while little terra-cotta figures are sculptural diversions.

Jean-Claude incorporated large stones into the design from the foundation of the dilapidated garage, which was

The fading leaves of *Hosta plantaginea* add a bittersweet glow to the bench in lovers' corner, above, one of several areas in the garden. Below: honeylocust and maiden grass near the back steps. The vine-covered trellis and gate opposite beckons one into the garden but ensures privacy. Top: a cultivar of *Cotoneaster dammerii*, and Boston ivy

removed to make room for the pergola; several slabs were used to create a bench in a shady corner, another distinct area. "Habib calls the bench the lovers' corner," says Cinea. Underplantings include: hostas, such as 'Big Daddy', which mellow to a buttery yellow in the autumn; ferns, such as the ostrich fern (*Matteuccia struthiopteris*); perennial geraniums, such as *Geranium* x *cantabrigiense* 'Biokova Karmina'; musk mallows (*Malva moschata*); and a row of orange tuberous begonias.

In another little garden room on the south side of the house, a small café table and two chairs nestle under one of the honeylocusts, which also turn a rich gold during the autumn, filtering the season's waning light.

Cinea keeps a collection of 120 tender tropical plants in her solarium throughout the winter. Every spring she moves about 20 pots into the garden. At strategic spots she has placed datura (*Brugmansia* spp.), crown of thorns (*Euphorbia milii*), cacti and bromeliads. A potted rosemary on the deck is a metre tall. The tender plants mingle happily with their hardier cousins, planted in the ground against the solarium's outside wall. A trumpet vine (*Campsis* x *tagliabuana*) climbs to the second floor windows, while a 'Constance Spry' rose scrambles up beside it as far as the first storey. At their feet are lady's-mantle (*Alchemilla mollis*) and sage.

Cinea has also incorporated sculptures into the garden. An artfully placed pedestal in the pond supports a pot of Christmas cacti (*Schlumbergera* x *buckleyi*) and the wings of a sculpture by San Francisco artist Phill Evans turn in the wind as water cascades down the sides.

There is an irony that has not escaped Cinea. In the past decade, she has gone from wondering why people bothered to plant gardens in cold countries to enjoying hers for a great part of the year. She retired two years ago and devotes a lot of her time to the garden. "I love the beginning of spring, when plants start to emerge after a couple of warm days. It's like a miracle," she says.

After four months in which her country is not a country, but winter, and her garden is not a garden, but snow, it is indeed a miracle. ∎

The pond is tucked under an edge of the low, two-level dining deck and is traversed with a plank path that leads to the pergola at the rear of the garden. Aquatic plants include flowering rush, narrow-leafed cattails and water hyacinth, plus a lush growth of waterlilies. Terra-cotta figures and unusual urns are used as sculptural diversions. Above: a summer view of the path to the deck seen on opening page

creating a pond

Water plants become established quickly and fill the surface of the pond with life in a few weeks, as seen in Dennis Eveleigh's pond, opposite. Above: arrowhead (*Sagittaria latifolia*), a plant for the margin of a pond

The thought of building a pond can intimidate even the most robust gardener or do-it-your-selfer, but here's one that was created in four days by an admitted semi-fit male of small stature, a father of two young boys who wanted an aquatic ecosystem for the children to observe. The goal was also to make a natural-looking pond that appeared to have been there for years, one that would enhance the family's Ontario garden.

"I also wanted first-hand experience building and maintaining a pond so I could teach people how to do it," says Dennis Eveleigh, who is a horticulturist at the Royal Botanical Garden in Burlington, Ontario. "I found the task challenging but not overwhelming, although digging out the soil made my underused muscles scream, and moving the rocks was a test of strength."

garden project

1

Dennis's pond is 1 metre wide, 2 metres long and 1 metre deep; it has an adjacent bog 1 metre wide, 60 centimetres long and 60 centimetres deep. To overwinter fish, a pond needs to be deep enough that the water does not freeze solid in winter: 60 centimetres is a minimum, but you may need to go 1.5 metres deeper in areas colder than southern Ontario. Check local bylaws before you dig. Ponds deeper than 60 centimetres may come under swimming pool regulations. Here's Dennis Eveleigh's advice on building a pond.

SITING AND PLANNING

Most water plants require sun to thrive, so a pond should be situated where it gets at least four hours of direct sunshine—the more, the better. Dennis sited his pond about a half-metre from a wooden fence on the west side of his garden, where it receives direct sun from 11 a.m. to 3 p.m. on most summer days (photo 1).

If you want to install a submersible pump to recirculate water for a fountain or water-fall, make sure an electric outlet is nearby.

Draw the layout of your yard on graph paper, identifying and measuring major features such as fences, walkways, trees, existing garden beds—and, of course, the buildings (including windows and doors) from where the pond will be viewed. The

location of underground gas lines and the like are important.

On pieces of tracing paper laid over the yard plan, try out several shapes for your proposed pond. After the final design is chosen, copy it onto the main plan. Then draw it life-size on a large sheet of paper (or use several sheets of paper taped together). Cut it out and place it on the pond site as a template.

GETTING THE SHAPE AND LEVEL RIGHT

Space stakes (such as 15-centimetre tent pegs), 50 centimetres apart, in the ground around the edges of the pattern (photo 2). At this point, it's important to level the stakes. Since the stakes will be used to ensure that the top edge of the pond is perfectly level, it's essential to be accurate with these measurements. Dennis placed a carpenter's level on the tops of two adjacent stakes, adjusted them, and then moved the level over one stake, adjusting it up or down (this method is shown in photo 3).

He continued this process around the pond, where minor adjustments were necessary to get the first and last stake to the

same level. To double-check, place a straight 2-x-4 board, longer than the pond at its widest point, on top of two stakes on either side of the pond, and then place the level on the board. Check several stakes across from each other until you're sure all the stakes are level. This will give you an accurate point of reference for all subsequent measurements and save a lot of time and trouble.

Dennis's site was not perfectly level, so the amount of stake exposed varied from one to another. With a measuring tape, he determined that the most exposed stake was 5 centimetres aboveground. So Dennis measured down 5 centimetres from the top of each stake and used a garden trowel to cut out a perfectly level top edge of the pond. Then he double-checked that the pond's edge was level, again using the carpenter's level and board.

DIGGING

With a square-mouth spade, carefully cut the edge of the pond just inside the row of stakes, cutting at a 45° angle and taking care not to disturb the edging soil. Use a round-mouth shovel to dig out the centre of the pond, piling the soil on a tarp next to the construction site (photo 4). Put fertile topsoil in one pile (to use in your garden later) and the lighter-coloured, less-fertile subsoil in a

Once the pond was dug, a small, shallower bog garden was made at one end of the pond. A section of soil is left between the pond and the bog to act as a dike yet allow water to spill over from pond to bog. Underpadding is shaped over the pond and bog, then the liner is positioned and anchored with rocks, and the pond is filled one-third with water. After the first layer of edging rocks are placed, more water is added. Far right: water forget-me-not

5

6

7

8

2   3   4

Dennis's pond was sited near a fence fronted by a perennial bed that had to be removed and the earth smoothed. Once the pond's shape was decided upon, a paper template was pegged in place. Levelling the pond is an ongoing process during construction, especially as it's being dug. After the pond edges are shaved down- ward with a square-mouth spade, the excavation is dug with a round-mouth shovel; levels to hold plants are sculpted with the trowel.

separate pile. If you hit subsoil mixed with gravel and rocks, as Dennis did after about 30 centimetres, use a garden fork along with the shovel.

As you progress, lay the 2 x 4 across the surface of the soil between the stakes and measure down from it as you dig. Use the spade and a trowel to sculpt 4-centimetre- wide shelves—two of them 30 centimetres down and one 60 centimetres down—for the potted marginal plants.

At the 75-centimetre depth, Dennis hit the water table, and water began seeping into the hole and remained at that depth as he dug. Dennis used a submersible pump wrapped in a sheet of landscape fabric to act as a filter to pump the water out.

"That evening there was a downpour, and the following morning my kids were excited because the pond was overflowing," says Dennis. "Rainwater from my yard and neighbouring yards was draining directly through the site. I pumped it out, and then dug a drainage channel between the pond and the fence. Later, I graded the soil so it

CONSTRUCTION SUPPLIES
two tarps
  (one to pile soil on, one to cover)
carpenter's level
straight piece of 2-x-4 wood longer
  than the pond at its widest point
wooden stakes or tent pegs, at least
  2.5 x 2.5 x 15 centimetres
  (enough to go around the
  pond's perimeter spaced
  50 centimetres apart)
the best-quality pond liner you can
  afford (rubber lasts longest and
  is the most puncture-resistant)
1-centimetre-thick foam carpet
  underpadding or fabric
  pond underlay
grey or black fabric pond underlay
flat rocks 2 to 5 centimetres thick
  (enough to cover edges with
  two layers)
submersible water pump and
  2 metres or more of plastic hose
small sheet of landscape fabric
outdoor extension cord
bog soil
garden soil
peat moss

GARDEN TOOLS YOU'LL NEED
round-mouth shovel
square-mouth spade
garden fork
garden hose attached to a tap
tooth rake
hand trowel
tape measure
scissors or garden shears
old bread knife

garden project

At right, the rocks are in place, the bog (upper end of pond) has been filled with a soil and peat moss mix, and the pond is topped up with water. All is ready for planting with, from top, black-eyed Susans, lobelia, marsh marigold and pickerel weed. Left: water lettuce

sloped away from the pond."

Next, dig out the bog area beside the pond, making sure the bog's edges are at the same height or higher than the pond's. Mark the perimeter of the size you plan with more stakes; then, using the square-mouth spade, dig a hole 60 centimetres deep with a 5-centimetre-deep shelf around the edge to hold the edging rocks. Leave a section of soil 30-centimetres wide between the pond and the bog to act as a dike—it will allow overflow from the pond to spill into the bog (photo 5 on page 212).

INSTALLING THE LINER

Check again to make sure the tops of the stakes are still level and pump out any water that may have seeped into the bottom of the pond. To make a shelf for the edging rocks, cut out a section 5-centimetres deep and about 15 centimetres wide around the top of the pond. Make sure it is level by checking

the stakes again. Before putting in the lining, remove sharp stones that may be in the bottom of the excavation. Line the pond and bog with a protective layer of used, 1-centimetre-thick foam carpet under-padding or fabric pond underpadding, available at most garden centres (photo 6). Cardboard or even a 1-centimetre layer of sand will also work.

Lay the folded rubber liner over the pond, carefully positioning the centre in the bottom of the hole. Take care not to stretch the liner as you unfold it and press it against the sides. A single piece of liner was used to cover the pond, dike and bog areas. To keep the liner as flat as possible, fold the excess and overlap the folds so that it's pleated. The liner should extend past the edges of the pond and bog by at least 30 centimetres.

To protect the rubber liner, lay a piece of fabric pond liner over it, again pleating it and allowing it to extend to the pond edges. Lay thin, flat rocks on the plant shelves and place several large rocks on the bottom of the pond to prevent the fabric from floating. Next, fill the pond two-thirds full with water to press the rubber liner firmly in place (photo 7).

Place a row of 5-centimetre-thick flat rocks on the 5-centimetre edging shelf, positioning them to overlap the pond edge by 2.5 centimetres (photo 8). Using scissors, cut off the foam underpadding just at the

outer edge of the rocks. Cut the rubber liner and fabric so that 8 centimetres extends beyond the outer edges of the rocks. Then fold the overhang over and on the top of the edging rocks all the way around the pond and bog. Place a second layer of rocks over the folded-over liner and fabric.

"It costs more to use a double row of rocks around the edge," says Dennis, "but it's well worth it. It's difficult to hide the liner at the water's edge with a single row, and an exposed liner looks artificial and can be damaged by sunlight." A double row, with the liner folded under the top layer, allows the pond's water level to come to the top of the first rock layer.

A word of caution: using limestone rocks may cause a water pH problem. Limestone can make the water very alkaline, which is harmful to plants and fish. Check with a pond-water test kit—a pH of 6.0 to 7.5 is desirable.

For the bog soil, prepare a 50/50 mix of garden soil and well-moistened peat moss. Fill the bog with this soil to the top of the lower row of rocks. Dig a small hole about 15 centimetres deep in the centre of the bog; then, using the garden hose, add enough water to create standing water in the shallow hole. If the soil shrinks once it's saturated, add more to bring it back to its original level (photo 9, top part of pond).

Next, fill the pond with water to the top of the lower row of rocks so it flows between the rocks on the dike and seeps into the bog (photo 9).

PLANTING BOG AND POND

Hand-digging holes for plants in the soft soil of the bog is easy. In the pond, carefully place marginal plants in black plastic pots on the sculpted shelves. A potted water plant, such as a waterlily, can be set on an overturned pot on the bottom of the pond to raise it closer to the surface until it grows bigger. Aerating plants, such as hornwort,

HOW TO CALCULATE LINER SIZE:
(pond depth x 2) + pond width + 60 centimetres = liner width
(pond depth x 2) + pond length + 60 centimetres = liner length

9

which are weighted to sink to the bottom, should be added—about six plants for a pond this size. Add a pailful of water containing floating duckweed, micro-organisms and tiny water creatures from a local wetland area to get the aquatic ecosystem started. The duckweed provides shade for the pond until the other water plants grow, and it can be removed later.

"For the sound of water, I placed a submersible water pump in the pond, with the plastic hose hidden around the edge and running up to the top of a large edging rock so water would run across the rock and trickle into the pond," Dennis says. To use a submersible pump you'll have to have an electrical outlet nearby. ▪

plants
forponds

SUBMERGED PLANTS (also known as aeration plants or aerators): plants that may or may not be rooted in the pond bottom, that grow entirely under the water; they don't actually aerate the water as much as they grab nutrients and prevent algae growth

Ceratophyllum demersum (hornwort)
(weighted with lead weights), Zone 8

DEEP-WATER PLANTS: plants rooted in soil, then placed in water deeper than 30 centimetres and grow with their leaves and flowers on or above the water surface

Nymphaea x *marliacea* 'Albida'
(waterlily), hardy

MARGINAL PLANTS: plants that grow in soil covered by several centimetres of water and grow up out of the water along the pond edge

Juncus articulatus (jointed rush), Zone 5
Juncus effusus (soft rush), Zones 4 to 6
Juncus inflexus (blue rush), Zone 9
Myriophyllum aquaticum
(parrot's feather), Zone 9
Nymphoides peltata (floating heart),
Zone 6
Pontederia cordata (pickerel weed),
Zone 3
Potentilla palustris (water strawberry),
Zone 3
Ranunculus flammula
(small creeping spearwort), Zone 5
Sagittaria latifolia (arrowhead), Zone 5
Typha minima (dwarf cattails), Zone 3

FLOATING PLANTS: plants that float on top of the water and are not rooted in soil

Lemna minor (duckweed), Zone 4
Pistia stratiotes (water lettuce)
(tender), Zone 9

BOG PLANTS: plants that grow in soil that is constantly moist, normally near a body of water; although they can briefly tolerate it, they prefer not to grow in soil constantly covered by water

Caltha palustris (marsh marigold),
Zone 3
Epimedium youngianum 'Niveum'
(barrenwort), Zone 5
Gentiana asclepiadea (willow gentian),
Zone 6
Houttuynia cordata, Zone 6
Iris sibirica (siberian iris), Zone 4
Iris versicolor (blue flag), Zone 3
Ligularia dentata 'Desdemona'
(big-leaf goldenray), Zone 4
Lobelia siphilitica (great blue lobelia),
Zone 5
Mentha aquatica (water mint), Zone 6
Mimulus guttatus
(common monkey flower), Zone 6
Myosotis scorpioides, *M. paulstris*
(water forget-me-not), Zone 5
Primula pubescens 'Exhibition Yellow'
(primrose), Zone 3
Astilboides tabularis
(Rodgersia tabularis), Zone 5
Trollius europaeus
(common globeflower), Zone 5 ■

Even just after planting, Dennis Eveleigh's pond looked established. It's important to use marginal plants to soften the edges of the rocks and to use plants that will tumble and swirl over the setting to make the pond look natural. Clockwise, from above: *Veronica repens* 'Sunshine'; *Iris versicolor*; *ligularia* 'The Rocket'; globeflower; the brand new pond; pickerel weed; *Sedum kamtschaticum*

index

Page numbers in **bold type** indicate photographs.

a

Acer (maple), 123, 126, 128, 152–54, 174, 186. See also *Acer palmatum*
Acer palmatum *(Japanese maple),* 14, 21, 48–50, 71, 196, 198
   A. dissectum palmatum (cutleaf Japanese maple), 25, 27, 116
Aconitum (monkshood), 87
Adam, Judith, 24–25
Adiantum pedatum (maidenhair fern), 70, 122
Aegopodium (goutweed), 47, 54
Agapanthus umbellatus (lily-of-the-Nile), 71, 114
Ajuga reptans (bugleweed), 27, 56
Akebia quinata (chocolate vine), 27, 56
Alchemilla (lady's-mantle), 30, 87, 119, 120, 208
Allium, 116
Alocasia (taro), 71, 111, 196
alyssum *(Lobularia maritima),* 46
Amelanchier, 27, 93
Ampelopsis brevipedunculata (porcelain vine), 144
Anemone, 85, 87, 117
Aquilegia (columbine), 27, 87, 139
arbours, 20, 136–37, 157
Arctostaphylos uva-ursi (bearberry), 27
Arisaema (Jack-in-the-pulpit), **80,** 155
Armstrong, Diana and Michael, 68–73
Artemisia, 76, 79, 119
Arthurs, Penny, 90–93, 130–31, 146–50
Arum italicum (lords and ladies), 15, 87
Aruncus aethusifolius (dwarf goatsbeard), 27, 56
Asarum canadense (wild ginger), 27, 155

Asclepias (butterfly weed), 87
Asiatic lily, 93, **154**
Aster, 174
Astilbe, 35, 36, 93, 117, 122
Astilboides tabularis, 216
Astrantia, 119
Aubrieta, 36
autumn fern *(Dryopteris erythrosora),* 27
azalea, 71, 112, 128, 174, 198

b

baby's-breath, 128
bamboo, 186
banana palm, 111
Baptisia lactea (white false indigo), 27
barrenwort *(Epimedium),* 87, 216
bayberry *(Myrica pensylvanica),* 126
bay tree, 43
bearberry *(Arctostaphylos uva-ursi),* 27
beard-tongue *(Penstemon),* 87
beautybush *(Kolkwitzia),* 76
Beder, Ralph, 18–21
bee balm, 84
beech *(Fagus),* 126
Begonia, 35, 46, **110,** 112, 208
bellflower *(Campanula),* 35, 36, 118, 124
Bergenia, 56, 111
berries, 30, 128
berry bladder fern *(Cystopteris bulbifera),* 27
Betula (birch), 21, 174, 192
bird of paradise *(Strelitzia reginae),* 111
bittersweet *(Celastrus),* 17, 206
bloodroot *(Sanguinaria),* 87
blue fescue *(Festuca glauca),* 21
blue flag *(Iris versicolor),* 216
blue flax, 124
blue oats *(Helictotrichon sempervirens),* 202
blue star creeper *(Isotoma fluviatilis),* 170
bog gardens, 36, 79, 125, 174, 212, 214–16
Bothern, Ruth, 88–93

Bougainvillea, 111, 112
boxwood *(Buxus),* 17, 27, 35, 37
brown-eyed Susan, 139
Brugmansia (datura), 71, 79, 111, 208
Brunnera, 118
Buddleia davidii (butterfly bush), 125, 142
bugleweed *(Ajuga reptans),* 27, 56
bulbs, 91, 116, 123, 148
burning bush *(Euonymus alata),* 17
Butomus umbellatus (flowering rush), 206, **209**
buttercup *(Ranunculus),* 56, 139, 216
butterfly bush *(Buddleia davidii),* 125, 142
butterfly weed *(Asclepias),* 87
butternut *(Juglans cinerea),* 122, 123
Buxus (boxwood), 17, 27, 35, 37

c

Calendula, 124
Calgary, 188–95
Calluna (heather), 116, 128
Caltha palustris (marsh marigold), 139, 174, 216
Campanula (bellflower), 35, 36, 118, 124
Campsis (trumpet vine), 208
Canna, 111
Caragana arborescens (Siberian peashrub), 48, 206
cardinal flower *(Lobelia cardinalis),* **117,** 119, 128
Carex, 202
carnation *(Dianthus),* **123,** 128, **136,** 139
Caryopteris, 157
catmint *(Nepeta),* 46, 87
cattail *(Typha),* 206, **209,** 216
cedar *(Thuja),* 37, 52, 54, 56, 128, 198
Celastrus (bittersweet), 17, 206
Ceratophyllum demersum (hornwort), 214–15, 216

Cercis (redbud), 155
Cerinthe major (honeywort), 116
Cestrum elegans, 119
Chaenomeles speciosa (flowering quince), 14, 198
Chamaecyparis (cypress), 52, 126, 180
Chasmanthium latifolium (northern sea oats), 27, 56, 202
chocolate vine *(Akebia quinata),* 27, 56
chokecherry *(Prunus virginiana),* 52, 123
Christmas cactus *(Schlumbergera* x *buckleyi),* 208
Christmas fern *(Polystichum acrostichoides),* 56
Christmas rose *(Helleborus niger),* 27, 116
Chrysanthemum, 128, 198
Cimicifuga, 27, 87
cinquefoil *(Potentilla),* 56, 124–25, 216
Clarke, Brian, 176–80
Clematis, 27, 87, 112, 117
   on trellises and arbours, 73, 82, 136–37, 185
   on walls and fences, 17, 93, 144, 157
Cleome (spider flower), **26–28,** 44
climbing hydrangea *(Hydrangea anomala petiolaris),* 17, 27, 65, **89,** 126
Cole, Trevor, 48, 50
Colocasia (elephant's ears), 111
columbine. See *Aquilegia*
coneflower. See *Echinacea; Rudbeckia*
container gardening, 43, 70–71, 79, 102–5, 149, 160–65. See also tropical plants
coralbells *(Heuchera),* 27, 35, 70, 76, 111
Coreopsis (tickseed), 14, 21, 87
corkscrew hazel *(Corylus avellana* 'Contorta'*),* 197
Cornus (dog-wood), 148, 199
   C. alba 'Sibirica' (Siberian dogwood), 144, 198
   C. alternifolia (pagoda dog

wood), 14, 25–27, 50
C. florida (flowering dogwood), 50, 71
C. kousa, 21, 50, **53,** 119, 149
yellow twig dogwood, 14, 198
Corydalis, 87
Corylus avellana 'Contorta' (corkscrew hazel), 197
Cosmos, 44, 119
costmary *(Tanacetum balsamita),* 79
Cotinus coggygria (purple smoke tree), 35, 37, 198
Cotoneaster, 149, 199, **206**
Cotula potentillina (New Zealand brass buttons), 170
crabapple *(Malus),* 50, 148, 149, 185
Craggs, Marilyn, 38
Crambe cordifolia (sea kale), 87
cranesbill *(Geranium),* 14, 76, 87, 116, 119, 208
Crassula ovata (jade plant), 111
creeping Jenny *(Lysimachia nummularia),* 54, 56, **82,** 170
Creighton, Laureen, 21
crocosmia, 111
crocus, 85, 199
crown of thorns (Euphorbia *milii),* 208
Culver's root *(Veronicastrum virginicum),* 87
Curcuma, 71
curry plant, 117
Cyclamen, 87, 191
cypress *(Chamaecyparis),* 52, 126, 180
Cystopteris bulbifera (berry bladder fern), 27

d
daffodil, 174
dahlia, 76
dame's rocket *(Hesperis matronalis),* 87
Daoud, Cinea de Souza and Habib, 204–8
Daphne, 14, 17, 27, 82, 85
Datura, 108. See also

Brugmansia
dawn redwood *(Metasequoia glyptostroboides),* 126
daylily *(Hemerocallis),* 17, 46, **144, 156,** 185–86
Delphinium, 14, 47, 87, **121,** 139
Deschampsia, 27, 116–17, 202
Dianthus (carnation), **123,** 128, **136,** 139
Dicentra (bleeding heart), 27, 36, **79,** 87
Dictamnus (gasplant), 87, 157
Digitalis (foxglove), **39, 70,** 79, 87
Dinnick, Brenda, 94–97
Dodecatheon meadia (shooting star), 87
dogwood. See *Cornus*
Doronicum (leopard's bane), 87, 192
Dryopteris erythrosora (autumn fern), 27
duckweed *(Lemna minor),* 216
Dyer, Geoffrey and Susan, 80–88

e
Echinacea purpurea (purple coneflower), 36, 44, 87
Edmonton, 120–25, 134–39
Eichhornia crassipes (water hyacinth), 71, 186, 196, 206, **209**
elder, 185–86
elephant's ears (Colocasia), 111
Epimedium (barrenwort), 87, 216
Eremurus robustus (foxtail lily), 87
Erica (heath), 128, 198
Eryngium alpinum (alpine sea holly), 87
Euonymus, 17, **94**
Eupatorium (Joe-Pye weed), 27, 87
Euphorbia (spurge), 15, 117, 119, 208
Eveleigh, Dennis, 210–15
evergreens, 36, 37, 116, 128, 185, 196

f
Fagus sylvatica (European beech), 126
false indigo *(Baptisia),* 27
Fatsia, 117
fennel, 128
ferns, 35, 36, 79, 111, 185, 196. See also specific varieties
Festuca glauca (blue fescue), 21
Filipendula (meadowsweet), 87
fish, 21, 179, 212
floating heart *(Nymphoides peltata),* 216
flowering almond *(Prunus triloba),* 17, 52
foamflower *(Tiarella),* 87, 155
Fort Erie (Ontario), 44–47
fountain grass *(Pennisetum alopecuroides),* 202
fountains, 64–65, 71, 91, 176
foxglove *(Digitalis),* **39, 70,** 79, 87
foxtail lily *(Eremurus robustus),* 87
Fuchsia, **39,** 119

g
Galium odoratum (sweet woodruff), 148, 155, 199
gardens. See also specific types
children and, 14, 160–66
construction materials in, 14, 137, 150
furnishings for, 60–61, 123, 130–31, 137
Japanese-style, 174–87, 196–203
mirrors in, 58–59, 98–101
gasplant *(Dictamnus),* 87, 157
Gaura lindheimeri, 157
gay-feather *(Liatris spicata),* 21, 36
Gentiana (gentian), 118, 216
Geranium (cranesbill), 14, 76, 87, 116, 119, 208
ginger *(Asarum canadense),* 27, 155
Gingko, 119
Gladiolus, 122
Gleditsia (honeylocust), 93, 206,

208
globeflower *(Trollius),* 122, **125,** 216
glorybush *(Tibouchina),* 71
goatsbeard *(Aruncus),* 27, 56
golden chain *(Laburnum watereri),* 52
goutweed *(Aegopodium),* 47, 54
grapevines, 30
grasses, ornamental, 196, 198, 199, 202–3. See also specific varieties
Gunnera manicata, 79, 108, 111

h
hair grass *(Deschampsia vivipara),* 27
Hakonechioa, 202
Hamamelis (witch hazel), 119
hawthorn, 128
heather *(Calluna),* 116, 218
heath *(Erica),* 128, 198
Hedera helix (English ivy), 56, 65
Helenium (sneezeweed), 87
Helianthus (sunflower), 87
Helictotrichon sempervirens (blue oats), 202
Helleborus (hellebore), 14, 27, 87, 112, 116, 174
Hemerocallis (daylily), 17, 46, **144, 156,** 185–86
hemlock *(Tsuga),* 155, 198
hens-and-chickens *(Sempervivum),* **161,** 192
Hepatica, 155
herbs, 15, 30, 42, 46, 76, 77–79
Herniaria glabra (rupturewort), 171
Herron, Gerry and FranCeen, 108–12
Hesperis matronalis (dame's rocket), 87
Heuchera (coralbells), 27, 35, 70, 76, 111
Hibiscus, 43, 44, 47, 71, 85, 111
hollyhock, 44
honeylocust *(Gleditsia),* 93, 206, 208
honey plant *(Melianthus major),*

index

117, 119
honeywort *(Cerinthe major),* 116
hornwort *(Ceratophyllum
    demersum),* 214–15, 216
Hosta, 15, 27, 70, 117, 198,
    208
Houttuynia cordata, 216
Hurni, Jean-Claude, 206–8
Hydrangea, 27, 112, 117–18,
    144, 148, 207
    H. anomala petiolaris (climb-
        ing hydrangea), 17, 27, 65,
        89, 126
    H. grandiflora 'Pee Gee,'
        14–15
    H. quercifolia (oakleaf
        hydrangea), 155
Hylotelephium, 119
Hypericum (St. John's wort), 87
hypertufa, 163–65

i

Imperata cylindrica (Japanese
    bloodgrass), 21, **117,** 202
Ipomoea (morning glory), **39,**
    112, **122**
Iris, 36, 44, 122, 128, 174, 186
    dwarf iris, 35
    I. sibirica (Siberian iris), 35,
        185, 216
    I. versicolor (blue flag), 216
Isotoma fluviatilis (blue star
    creeper), 170
ivy, 35, 93, 112, 136–37. See
    also Hedera helix

j

Jack-in-the-pulpit *(Arisaema),*
    80, 155
Jacob's ladder *(Polemonium),* 27
jade plant *(Crassula ovata),* 111
Japanese beech fern
    *(Thelypteris decursive-
    pinnata),* 27
Japanese bloodgrass *(Imperata
    cylindrica),* 21, **117,** 202
Japanese maple. See *Acer
    palmatum*
jasmine, flowering, 174
Joe-Pye weed *(Eupatorium),* 27,

87
Jones, Cathy, 152–58
Juglans cinerea (butternut tree),
    122, 123
Juncus (rush), 186, 216
Juniperus (juniper), 37, 124–25,
    191, 195, 198
    J. scopulorum, 52, 185
pruning, 180

k

Kalmia (mountain laurel), 128
Kelowna, 108–12
Kemp, Steve and Annie, 18–21
Kentucky coffee tree, 128
Kerria japonica, 198
Kirengeshoma palmata (yellow
    wax-bells), 87, 117
Kitchener, 74–79
Kniphofia (red-hot poker), 87
Kolkwitzia (beautybush), 76

l

Labrador tea *(Ledum
    groenlandicum),* 139
Labrador violet *(Viola
    labradorica),* 170
Laburnum watereri (golden
    chain), 52
ladyslipper orchid, 71
lady's-mantle *(Alchemilla),* 30,
    87, 119, 120, 208
lamb's-ears *(Stachys byzantina),*
    36, **39,** 46, 76, 117, 139
Langen, Terie, 30
Langley, Joan, 120–25
Laptinella potentillina (New
    Zealand brass buttons), 170
larch, 198
Lathyrus (pea), 15, 39, 82, 87, 128
Latimer, Michael, 178–79
Laurentia fluviatilis. See *Isotoma
    fluviatilis*
Lavatera (mallow), 87, 112, 122
lavender, 15, 43, 46, 116
leadwort *(Plumbago),* 71
Ledum groenlandicum (Labrador
    tea), 139
Lemna minor (duckweed), 216
Lenten rose *(Helleborus*

oriental is), 87, 116
leopard's bane *(Doronicum),* 87,
    192
Liatris, 21, 36
Ligularia, 120, 122, 216
Ligustrum (privet), 14, 35
lilac *(Syringa),* 17, 93, 144, 148,
    190, 195
lily, 30, 82, 122, 123, 128. See
    also specific varieties
lily-of-the-Nile (Agapanthus
    umbellatus), 71, **114**
lily-of-the-valley, **77,** 128, 192
Lily tigrinum (tiger lily), **15,** 38
linden, 125
Lindsay, Ann and David, 40–43
Lobelia, **117,** 119, 128, 216
Lobularia maritima (sweet
    alyssum), 46
Lombardy poplar, 119
London (Ontario), 40–44
Lonicera (honeysuckle), 15, 73,
    82, 85, 117, 136–37
lords and ladies *(Arum italicum),*
    15, 87
lungwort *(Pulmonaria),* 87
lupine, 128, 139
Lychnis coronaria (rose
    campion), 87
Lysimachia, 54, 56, **82,**
    117, 170

m

Magnolia, 14, 65, 71
maiden grass *(Miscanthus),* 21,
    111, 202, **207**
maidenhair fern *(Adiantum
    pedatum),* 70, 122
mallow *(Lavatera),* 87, 112, 122
Malus (flowering crabapple), 50,
    148, 149, 185
Malva moschata (musk mallow),
    208
Mandevilla, 70, 71
maple. See *Acer*
Marmina, Joel, 198–201
Marmina, Joseph and Paulie,
    196–203
Marmina, Michael, 198–99
marsh marigold *(Caltha
    palustris),* 139, 174, 216

martagon lily, 123
Matteuccia struthiopteris (ostrich
    fern), 208
Maxwell, Lily and Glenn, 114–19
Mayday tree *(Prunus padus),*
    124–25
Mazus reptans (creeping
    mazus), 171
meadowrue *(Thalictrum),* 27
meadowsweet *(Filipendula),* 87
Melianthus major (honey plant;
    peanut butter plant), 117,
    119
Mertensia virginica (Virginia
    bluebells), 87
Metasequoia glyptostroboides
    (dawn redwood), 126
Millereau, Régis, 206
Mimulus guttatus (common
    monkey flower), 216
mint *(Mentha),* **177,** 216
Miscanthus (maiden grass), 21,
    111, 202, **207**
mock orange *(Philadelphus),* 27,
    124–25
moneywort *(Lysimachia
    nummularia),* 54, 56, **82,** 170
monkey flower *(Mimulus
    guttatus),* 216
monkshood *(Aconitum),* 87
Montgomery, Sunny and Peter,
    140–44
Montreal, 204–9
morning glory *(Ipomoea),* **39,**
    112, **122**
Morus *(mulberry),* 50, 91, 196
moss. See *Sagina*
mountain ash *(Sorbus
    americana),* 136, 192
mountain laurel *(Kalmia),* 128
mulberry *(Morus),* 50, 91, 196
mulch, 157, 201
Mumford, Joanne and Dave,
    182–87
Murray, Richard, 21
musk mallow *(Malva moschata),*
    208
Myosotis scorpioides (water
    forget-me-not) **211,** 216
Myrica pensylvanica (bayberry),
    126
Myriophyllum aquaticum

(parrot's feather), 216

n

Nepeta (catmint), 46, 87

New Zealand brass buttons
(*Cotula potentillina*), 170

New Zealand flax (*Phormium tonax*), 111

Novak, Jiri, 134–39

Nymphaea (waterlily), 21, 125, 206, 214, 216

Nymphoides peltata (floating heart), 216

o

oak (*Quercus*), 52, 128, 136

ostrich fern (*Matteuccia struthiopteris*), 208

p

Papaver orientale (Oriental poppy), 44, 47, 87, **136,** 139

parrot's feather (*Myriophyllum aquaticum*), 216

Parthenocissus quinquefolia (Virginia creeper), 17

pasqueflower (*Pulsatilla vulgaris*), 36, 87

Passiflora (passionflower), 112

paths, 25, 55–57, 166–71

patios, 25, 71, 185

peach, 192

peanut butter plant (*Melianthus major*), 117, 119

pear (*Pyrus*), 14, 24–25, 27

Pennisetum alopecuroides (fountain grass), 202

Penstemon (beard-tongue), 87

peony, 15, 71, 76, 125, 149

periwinkle (*Vinca minor*), 155

Perovskia atriplicifolia (Russian sage), 30

Perry, Val, 38

Persian lilac (*Syringa persica*), 190, 195

pH, 128, 214

Phalaris, 203

Philadelphus (mock orange), 27, 124–25

Phlox, 30, 44, 84, 87, 128, 154

Phormium tenax (New Zealand flax), 111

Phyllitis scolopendrium (hart's-tongue fern), 56

Picea (spruce), 191
blue spruce, 71, 196, 199
P. glauca var. albertiana (dwarf Alberta spruce), 35, 37, 52, 126
P. omorika (Serbian spruce), 52, 126

pickerel weed (*Pontederia cordata*), 174, 216

Pieris japonica, 17, 27

pincushion flower (*Scabiosa caucasica*), 87

Pinus (pine), 128, 180, 185, 198, 206
Scotch pine, 122, 125, 185

Pistia stratiotes (water lettuce), 21, 71, 206, **214, 216**

pitcher plant (*Sarracenia purpurea*), 79

planters. See container gardening

plants
drought-resistant, 157
dwarf, 35
for ponds, 216–17
and soil pH, 128
tropical, 21, 43, 71, 108–13, 196, 208

plum, **115,** 144

Plumbago (leadwort), 71

Polemonium (Jacob's ladder), 27

Polygonatum (Solomon's-seal), 27, 154

Polygonum aubertii (silver-lace vine), 20, 73, 144

Polystichum acrostichoides (Christmas fern), 56

ponds, 21, 79, 139, 186, 196, 206
building, 210–15
fish in, 21, 179, 212
plants for, 216–17

Pontederia cordata (pickerel weed), 174, 216

poplar, 119, 136

poppy, 118, 124. See also *Papaver orientale; Romneya coulteri*

porcelain vine (*Ampelopsis brevipedunculata*), 144

potato vine (*Solanum jasminoides*), 71

Potentilla (cinquefoil), 56, 124–25, 216

Primula (primrose), 27, 36, 87, 192, 218

privet (*Ligustrum*), 14, 35

pruning, 35, 37, 179, 180, 192

Prunus
P. padus (Mayday tree), 124–25
P. triloba (flowering almond), 17, 52
P. virginiana (chokecherry), 52, 123

Pulmonaria (lungwort), 87

Pulsatilla vulgaris (pasqueflower), 36, 87

purple bell vine (*Rhodochiton atrosanguineum*), 111

Pyrus (pear), 14, 24–25, 27

q

Quercus (oak), 52, 128, 136

quince, flowering (*Chaenomeles speciosa*), 14, 198

r

Ranunculus (buttercup), 56, 139, 216

redbud (*Cercis*), 155

red-hot poker (*Kniphofia*), 87

redwood, dawn (*Metasequoia glyptostroboides*), 126

Regina, 182–87

Reville, David, 152–58

Rheum (rhubarb), 111, 128

Rhodochiton atrosanguineum (purple bell vine), 111

Rhododendron, 71, 116, 125, 128, 174, 198

rhubarb (*Rheum*), 111, 128

ribbon grass, 122

Roberts, Susan, 134–39

rock gardens, 116–17, 188–95

Rodgersia, 27, 112, 216

Romneya coulteri (California tree poppy), 117

rose campion (*Lychnis coronaria*), 87

rose-of-Sharon (*Hibiscus syriacus*), 44, 47, 85

Rosa (rose), 17, 71, 142, 148, 149, 157
climbing, 15, **34,** 43, 73
David Austin, 44, 125, 157
Explorer, 27, 36, 43
R. 'Bonica,' 144, 149
R. 'Carefree Beauty,' 36
R. 'Constance Spry,' 157, 208
R. 'F. J. Grootendorst,' 43, 191
R. glauca, 27
R. 'Heritage,' 44
R. moyesii 'Nevada,' 84
R. 'Mrs. John Laing,' 27
R. 'New Dawn,' 117, 149
R. 'Royal Sunset,' 117
R. rugosa, 27, 43
R. 'Seafoam,' **88,** 90, 93
for tough conditions, 42, 43
wild, 191

Rudbeckia (coneflower), 21, 87

rue (*Ruta graveolens*), 36, 76, 77, 117

rupturewort (*Herniaria glabra*), 171

rush. See *Butomus umbellatus; Juncus*

Russian sage (*Perovskia atriplici folia*), 30

Ruta graveolens (rue), 36, 76, 77, 117

s

sage, **77,** 119, 208. See also *Perovskia atriplicifolia; Salvia*

Sagina (moss), 196, 198
S. subulata 'Aurea' (Scotch moss), 27, 170
S. subulata (Irish moss), 27, 170

Sagittaria latifolia (arrowhead), **210,** 216

St. John's wort (*Hypericum*), 87

Salix (willow), 27, 140, 190, 192

Salvia, 36, 87, 93, 139

Sanguinaria (bloodroot), 87

Santolina, 117

Sarracenia purpurea (pitcher

index

plant), 79
Saskatoon berry *(Amelanchier alnifolia)*, 27
Scabiosa caucasica (pincushion flower), 87
Schizostylis coccinea (kaffir lily), 174
Schlumbergera x *buckleyi* (Christmas cactus), 208
Schrader, William, 188–95
sea holly *(Eryngium)*, 87
sea kale *(Crambe cordifolia)*, 87
sea oats *(Chasmanthium latifolium)*, 27, 56, 202
Sedum, 35, 36, 85, 171, 191, 199
Sempervivum, **161**, 192, **196**
serviceberry *(Amelanchier canadensis)*, 93
shasta daisy, 36, 44, 124, 139
shelters, 60–63
Shim, Brigitte, 62–63
shooting star *(Dodecatheon meadia)*, 87
Shuttleworth, Erica, 12–17
Shuttleworth, Susan, 12–14
silver-lace vine *(Polygonum aubertii)*, 20, 73, 144
Smilacina racemosa (false Solomon's-seal), 155
Smith, Andrew, 88–93
smoke tree *(Cotinus coggygria)*, 35, 37, 198
sneezeweed *(Helenium)*, 87
snowberry *(Symphoricarpos albus)*, 126
snowdrops, 116, 154
Solanum jasminoides (potato vine), 71
Solenostemon, 112
Solomon's-seal *(Polygonatum)*, 27, 154. See also *Smilacina racemosa*
Sophora japonica, 27
Sorbus americana (mountain ash), 136, 192
southernwood *(Artemisia abrotanum)*, 79
spearwort *(Ranunculus flammula)*, 216
speedwell *(Veronica)*, 35, 36, 37, 170, **216**

Spencer, Patti and John, 44–47
spider flower *(Cleome)*, **26–28,** 44
Spiraea, 27, 124–25, 142
spruce. See *Picea*
spurge *(Euphorbia)*, 15, 117, 119, 208
Stachys byzantina (lamb's-ears), 36, **39**, 46, 76, **117,** 139
Stewartia pseudocamellia, 119
stonecrop *(Sedum)*, 35, **161,** 171, 191
stones
  as design elements, 71, 177–78, 207–8
  for paths, 25, 71, 166–67
  in rock gardens, 191, 195, 199, 201
  in water features, 177–78, 214
  streams, 121–25, 176–79
  dry, 185–86, **193,** 198–99
Strelitzia reginae (bird of paradise), 111
sunflower, **39,** 87
Sutcliffe, Howard, 62–63
sweet alyssum *(Lobularia maritima)*, 46
sweet pea *(Lathyrus odoratus)*, 15, 39, 82, 128
sweet woodruff *(Galium odoratum)*, 148, 155, 199
Symphoricarpos albus (snowberry), 126
Syringa (lilac), 17, 93, 144, 148, 190, 195

t
Tanacetum, 46, 79
taro *(Alocasia)*, 71, 111, 196
Taxus (yew), 37, 70, 71, 128, 196, 198
  T. media, 27
  T. x *media* 'Hillii' (Hill's yew), 56
Thalictrum (meadowrue), 27
Thelypteris decursive-pinnata (Japanese beech fern), 27
Thuja (cedar), 37, 52, 54, 56, 128, 198
Thymus (thyme), 27, 46, 142,

171, 186, 198
Tiarella (foamflower), 87, 155
Tibouchina (glorybush), 71
tickseed *(Coreopsis)*, 14, 21, 87
tiger lily *(Lily tigrinum)*, **15,** 38
toad lily *(Tricyrtis hirta)*, **15,** 87
Toronto, 140–59, 196–203
  classic gardens in, 68–73, 80–93
  small gardens in, 12–21, 32–37, 64–65
trees, 14, 48–53, 126
trellises, 14, 28, 56, 73, 76, 157
Tricyrtis hirta (toad lily), **15,** 87
Trillium, 155, **157**
Trollius (globeflower), 122, **125,** 216
tropical plants, 21, 43, 71, 108–13, 196, 208
trumpet lily, 142
trumpet vine *(Campsis)*, 208
Tsuga (hemlock), 155, 198
Tulipa (tulip), 157, 191, 199
Turnbull, Neil, 126
Typha (cattail), 206, **209,** 216

u
umbrella plant, 21
Unionville (Ontario), 22–29

v
Vancouver, 174–81
vegetables, 77, 128
Veronica (speedwell), 35, 36, 37, 170, **216**
Veronicastrum virginicum (Culver's root), 87
Viburnum, 17, 76, 85, 174
Victoria (B.C.), 114–19
Vinca minor (periwinkle), 155
Viola (violet), 54, 87, 170
Virginia bluebells *(Mertensia virginica)*, 87
Virginia creeper *(Parthenocissus quinquefolia)*, 17

w
Walter, Bill, 174–80
water conservation, 46

water features. See fountains; ponds; streams
water forget-me-not *(Myosotis scorpioides)*, **211,** 216
water gardens, 176–77
water hyacinth *(Eichhornia crassipes)*, 71, 186, 196,206, **209**
water lettuce *(Pistia stratiotes)*, 21, 71, 206, 214, 216
waterlily *(Nymphaea)*, 21, 125, 206, **214,** 216
water mint *(Mentha aquatica)*, 216
water strawberry *(Potentilla palustris)*, 216
wax-bells *(Kirengeshoma palmata)*, 87, 117
Weigela, 35, 37, 112
wild ginger *(Asarum canadense)*, 27, 155
Williams, Mike, 42
Williams, Pam, 32–37
willow *(Salix)*, 27, 140, 190, 192
Winnipeg, 30–31, 38–39
wisteria, 15, 71, 112, 174
witch hazel *(Hamamelis)*, 119
woolly thyme *(Thymus pseudolanuginosus)*, 171, 196
wormwood *(Aremisia)*, 76, 119

y
yarrow, 149
yew. See *Taxus*

z
Zakuta, Leo and Annette, 80
Zinnia, 76

contributors

The editors and publishers sincerely thank the following people for contributing to this book. Without knowledgeable authors who care about the gardens and gardeners they write about, and photographers willing to spend hours waiting to capture the gardens at their very best, *City Gardens* would not have been possible.

And a special thank you to the gardeners themselves, the people on the front lines. They plan, dig, plant and weed through cold, drought, rain and heat to achieve gardens for us all to appreciate.

gardens

Judith Adam: Classic Gardens, 80
Suzanne Anderton: Perennial Gardens, 108
Shirley Blevins: Classic Gardens, 68; Serenity Gardens, 174
Alain Charest: Classic Gardens, 74
Christine Dirks: Small Gardens, 40
Beckie Fox: Small Gardens, 22
Margaret Hryniuk: Serenity Gardens, 182
Laura Langston: Perennial Gardens, 114
Patricia Maitland: Small Gardens, 32
Paul Marshman: Small Gardens, 44; Serenity Gardens, 196
Marilynn McAra: Family Gardens, 134
Aldona Satterthwaite: Small Gardens, 12
Kathy Vey: Family Gardens, 140
Eva Weidman: Small Gardens, 30, 38
Stephanie Whittaker: Serenity Gardens, 204
Pamela Young: Small Gardens, 18; Classic Gardens, 88; Family Gardens, 146, 152
Suzanne Zwarun: Perennial Gardens, 120; Serenity Gardens, 188

illustrations

Erica Shuttleworth: Small Gardens, 14
Bonnie Summerfeldt-Boisseau: Small Gardens, 46, 56; Classic Gardens, 76, 94; Perennial Gardens, 123; Family Gardens, 136, 149; Serenity Gardens, 179, 198

photographs

Paul Bailey: Perennial Gardens, 114
Harrison Baker: Family Gardens, 171
Barrett & Mackay: Serenity Gardens, 217 centre left
Mark Bolton: Perennial Gardens, 127 bottom right
Jocelyn Boutin: Small Gardens, 49 top
Mark Burstyn: Small Gardens, 54
Chris Campbell: Classic Gardens, 104–105
Alain Charest: Classic Gardens, 74
Trevor Cole: Small Gardens, 52
Tracy Cox: Family Gardens, 167–169
Janet Davis: Small Gardens, 59 top
Christopher Dew: p.v, Small Gardens, 44; Perennial Gardens, 129; Classic Gardens, 88
Dennis Eveleigh: Serenity Gardens, 210 (pond photography only)
Andrew Farquhar: Perennial Gardens, 108
Anne Gordon: Perennial Gardens, 127 top right and bottom left
Patricia Holdsworth: Serenity Gardens, 182
Kathryn Hollinrake: Small Gardens, 18, 32; Classic Gardens, 80
Jean-Claude Hurni: Small Gardens, 49 bottom, 51 top right; Serenity Gardens, 204, 217 centre right
Bert Klassen: Small Gardens, 22, 40, 98; Classic Gardens, 104 left; Family Gardens, 134, 154; Serenity Gardens, 196
Richard Lavertue: Small Gardens, 51 bottom left
Debby Lytle: Family Gardens, 170
Marilynn McAra: Small Gardens, 59 bottom; Perennial Gardens, 120; Family Gardens, 142; Serenity Gardens, 188, 210, 214
Guy McCrum: Family Gardens, 148
Richard Palanuk: Small Gardens, 30, 38
Jerry Pavia: Serenity Gardens, 213 bottom, 215 centre left and right, 216, 217 top
Aleksandra Szywala: Small Gardens, 50, 51 top left, bottom right, 53
Nance Trueworthy: Serenity Gardens, 215 left middle
Paddy Wales: Serenity Gardens, 174
Roger Yip: Small Gardens, 12, 60, 62, 64; Classic Gardens, 68, 94, 103 top right; Family Gardens, 160, 164–166; Perennial Gardens, 130

projects and style ideas

Judith Adam: Perennial Gardens, 126
Trevor Cole: Small Gardens, 48
Yvonne Cunnington: Small Gardens, 58; Classic Gardens, 98, 100
Dennis Eveleigh: Serenity Gardens, 210, 216
Beckie Fox: Small Gardens, 43, 54
Karen Kirk: Small Gardens, 60, 62; Classic Gardens, 102
Laura Langston: Family Gardens, 163
Wendy LeBlanc: Family Gardens, 166
Mary Lynn O'Shea: Family Gardens, 102, 168
Jen Robson-Crespi: Family Gardens, 162
Christina Selby: stacked pots, 160
Merike Weiler: Small Gardens, 64; Classic Gardens, 94; Perennial Gardens, 126, 130

editors

Liz Primeau has been gardening since she was a suburban mother in her twenties, when she would escape to the petunia patch for a few minutes of horticultural therapy. Her pursuit of the perfect garden continued after she began working as an editor and writer for such magazines as *Toronto Life, Chatelaine* and *City Woman*, and reached obsessive proportions after she joined *Canadian Gardening* as its first editor in 1990. In 2000 she returned to the petunia patch but continues to write, speak at garden shows and seminars, and edit books such as this one. Her own most recent bestselling books are *The Cook's Garden* and *Front Yard Gardens*.

Aldona Satterthwaite learned about the joys of gardening from her grandmother and has developed six city gardens of her own. Her career has taken her from magazines to advertising to museums and back to magazines. Prior to joining *Canadian Gardening* as its editor, she was director of writing services at The Museum of Modern Art, New York. Aldona completed her journalism studies at the Regent Street Polytechnic in London, England, studied landscape architecture at Ryerson University and trained as a master gardener at the Civic Garden Centre, Toronto. She is the author of the guidebook to Royal Botanical Gardens in Burlington.